Innovate. Impact. Protect.

Join the innovator in the wireless industry!

You've helped protect our freedom and secure our nation. We thank you. Now, you can use your cybersecurity expertise to protect our people, networks and data at T-Mobile.

We're shaking up the wireless industry by delivering great experiences, products and service to our consumers. It's not just about the network, mobile devices and plans. We're also focused on staying ahead of the curve in terms of cybersecurity.

Join us and drive your career and find your passion as you experience great rewards and work with cutting edge technology!

We currently have the following opportunities available:

- Sr. Security Architect
- Principal Security Architect
- Information Security Manager

We're seeking bright individuals with expertise in the following areas:

- Governance/Risk/Compliance — Compliance SOX, CPNI, PCI, technology risk and remediation
- Security Solutions — Architecture and design consultation, mobile and product security
- CIRT/Security Operations — Operational oversight of security tools and systems, vulnerability management, data loss prevention, cyber incident response
- Information Security Management — Threat and vulnerability assessment, proactive threat detection and response

Break the mold, find your passion and enjoy some of our benefits:

- Competitive pay
- Medical, dental, vision coverage
- Generous paid time off
- Tuition Reimbursement
- Educational Assistance
- Employee Stock Purchase Plan
- Company matched 401(k)
- 10 discounted phone lines
- Exceptional long-term growth potential

Visit us at the 19th Colloquium for Information Systems Security Education and hear William Boni, our Vice President & Corporate Information Security Officer, on June 17th at 10:45am share his perspective and describe the incredible opportunities in information security with T-Mobile.

Learn more by visiting **www.tmobile.jobs**.

tmobile.jobs   **T · ·Mobile·**

 Join the careers conversation at: **#BeMagenta**

The Colloquium for Information System Security Education (CISSE) Special Edition:

Educational Approaches to Transition Former Military Personnel into the Cybersecurity Field, Spring 2015

CISSE Edition 2, Issue 2

The Colloquium for Information Systems Security Education (CISSE).

Please contact us at askCISSE@cisse.info

www.cisse.info

Table of Contents

Editor's Note

The Colloquium for Information System Security Education (CISSE) has represented the constant in the changing field of cybersecurity education. CISSE was established in 1996. Its mission was (and still is) to provide the single authoritative forum for conducting meaningful dialogue between the wide range of government, industry, and academic entities, which are involved in the protection of our nation's information and its information and communication technology assets.

All of the communities of interest who participate in CISSE's workshops, academic and roundtable presentations receive direct advice from government, industry and other experienced educators about how to develop and deploy effective cybersecurity curricula. The Community meets every year at CISSE in order to learn about and further discuss the most effective means of maintaining a high standard of excellence in practice in cybersecurity education.

There are also a significant number of pure academic papers, which are presented as part of the CISSE conference. In order to have any credibility as a source of new and evolving knowledge it is important that the highest academic standards apply to the presentation of new knowledge to the membership. Thus the papers submitted to the conference undergo double blind refereeing process and the best of the best get exposure in individual sessions.

These sessions reflect the best possible scholarship in the field of cybersecurity and are highly competitive. The most outstanding scholarship is then subsequently published in the Journal of the Conference. Given that background it should be understood that this is a special edition of the Journal of the Colloquium for Information Systems Security Education (CISSE). The ideas contained in this Journal represent the best thinking in the methods and practices for integrating veterans into the cybersecurity workforce.

The idea of tapping the existing pool of already highly skilled veterans for work in the field of cybersecurity is almost too obvious. Nonetheless, there are a number of systemic and cultural challenges that have to be overcome before this can take place. The general explication of what is required is outlined and discussed in the articles that are presented here.

The articles in this Journal address ways to more effectively leverage recent members of the military in order to ensure efficient integration of veterans into the cybersecurity workforce. And it is a particularly obvious and justified way to ensure a pipeline of high quality skilled cybersecurity researchers, and cybersecurity professionals for the future workforce.

Effective strategies for veteran education requires understanding the status of the existing communities of practice within the educational landscape, which is much more complex than people appreciate. Because the cultures of each of these communities of practice are so different, the awareness, training and education approach needs vary. The contents of this Journal focus on developing and maintaining a deep pool of talented veterans to serve the critical need for cybersecurity professionals. It will present and discuss an up-to-date set of approaches to ensuring a continuously capable workforce and it will present best practices for practical recruitment education and retention of trained cybersecurity professionals.

What you will find in this issue are 11 carefully selected papers that discuss aspects of how to bring recent military veterans into the mainstream. The articles here represent many avenues of thought. It is our considered opinion that this sort of wide-ranging dialogue constitutes the first steps in overcoming existing hurdles for veterans and it takes the first steps in ensuring that cybersecurity education will evolve into the kind of main tent attraction that we all want it to be. We would not have been able to do this alone, and so we would like to acknowledge Tamara Shoemaker for her outstanding work in managing the review process, and our colleagues who served as reviewers for this issue.

Co-Editors of this CISSE Special Edition:

Dan Shoemaker, Ph.D.
Professor, University of Detroit Mercy

Barbara Endicott-Popovsky, Ph.D.
Professor, University of Washington
Institute of Technology

Forward by: Susan C. Kemnitzer Deputy Division Director, CBET, National Science Foundation

The first GI bill provided education to 450,000 engineers, 14 Nobel Prize winners and three Presidents. As a society, we should achieve the same result with the post-9/11 veteran's educational benefit.

In August 2009, the U.S. Department of Veterans Affairs (VA) launched the implementation of new legislation to expand educational benefits for veterans of the U.S. armed forces who served on active duty after September 1, 2001. At the same time, experts reported serious concerns about the future adequacy of the U.S. engineering and science workforce. The post-9/11 veteran's educational benefit opened the door to an unparalleled opportunity for the United States to expand its technical workforce while serving those who served. Post-9/11 veterans include a diverse and pre-qualified pool of future talent for the nation's engineering and science employers; 15 percent are women and over 30 percent are underrepresented minorities. The new benefit will expand the financial opportunities available to help them pursue their post-secondary education. Ushering them into technical fields and shaping them into workforce-ready engineers and scientists, will require a wider community of partnerships among the veterans themselves, the nation's educational institutions, technology firms, the government's technical and scientific organizations, and others. To jumpstart the process, NSF's Division of Engineering Education and Centers sponsored a workshop on April 13-14, 2009 and implemented a small start-up grant program to assist engineering schools in an effort to attract and serve veterans. Several of these projects focus on preparing veterans for career in computer science and in particular cyber-security.

So I commend the Colloquium for Information System Security and Education for gathering idea, evidence and best practices on Educational Approaches to Transition Former Military Personnel into the Cybersecurity

Field (and other STEM disciplines). The wide range of topics contained in this issue is important individually but must be interconnected into a full range of services for veteran students. Success is dependent on a portfolio of factors and student veterans deserve support in all of them. This support must come from collaboration among academia, government and industry. Through this issue the Colloquium for Information System Security and Education is a key resource for foster this collaboration.

Thank you.

Susan Kemnitzer
National Science Foundation

Advocacy Partnered with Adult Educational Principles: An Educator's Personal Ethnography

Timothy Hideharu Anthony Ema
BS, ADN, MEd,
Doctoral Student in Education
University

Andragogy's (adult education principles) role in learner centered environment: an informal look at my journey from youth to a successful faculty instructor in a public school district high school to a graduate student in education and professional presenter / facilitator.

INTRODUCTION

Where to start first, I wasn't really sure but I knew I had to start looking at background information and literature. I started by asking questions: What is advocacy really and what made computer classes so different from other classes or courses of study? Technology is where I learned much of my instructor student interaction. Then I started looking at my own timeline and how I had to work for my own benefits. I had to start asking myself, "Where have I gone when it comes to needing another voice to speak for me or am I out there alone?" Next I began looking for definitions that I could justify and back with the literature and understand how the theme fit. A major question that I didn't foresee was that the manner and demeanor of the instructors of computer technology classes seemed very different from the attitudes and other main stream content rich undergraduate courses from more well established departments or subject areas. These courses were more geared to content dissemination and less about learner centered understanding and application. This is where computer technology classes clearly had a major difference, in that their concern was that the learner needed to really understand and apply materials and information that they were learning and making it more their own learning and knowledge base to draw from. From their new anchored knowledge, the student learner could apply their understanding to problems and situations that they face in their workplace and create the necessary applications to make a solution or an alternative conclusion as their training and education allows. This more inquiry approach to solving immediate issues is part andragogy (adult education principles) and pedagogy and a very interesting mixture.

PERSONAL BACKGROUND ON ADVOCACY IN MY FAMILY

Actually 31 years ago, the then South Side Journal, a local community newspaper, did an article on my father with a small amount on my mother. It has been framed and posted for many years in my brother's hair salon and is very impressive to look at my dad and brother 31 years ago. I never paid it much attention hanging in that picture frame in the salon, even though as a younger man I had read it many times in the past when it first came out, I had not actually thought much about it since the last time I read it many years ago. But now as I continued to care for my dad in his waning health, I looked up on the wall and began to reread the article again. There was no big surprise except that I was now writing a piece on advocacy and realized that advocacy permeates my whole family. My dad was a dentist and a Boy Scout leader for many decades much later in his life and I believed that the article focused on his advocacy and facilitating role that extends for most of his life and was reflected in the article or so I thought. But that is not what the article was about. As I reread the article more closely and with a better understanding, the article spoke about my father's patriotism and little if any bitterness for being interred in as an enemy national in his own country. As an American citizen my father and his remaining family members were transported by soldiers to a concentration camp in Arkansas during the 1941-1942 timeframe after the bombing of Pearl Harbor since my dad is Japanese American. It was hard for them as a family since they had just buried his father a few months earlier. It didn't matter that he was born here and that he is an American citizen; he and my aunt and grandmother were all placed into the camps. His time there was thankfully short due in part and in its entirety to a Professor Beale who is identified in the article as one of a team of professors that toured the Japanese

American internment camps and literally "rescued", the students in each of the camps that were medical or dental students. It was through their intervention that these students were allowed to return to a college or university that would accept them and continue their schooling. Much of what occurred in the camps was obscured over time but many of those that lived in these camps were living very different, very demeaning and very harsh lives. So yes my dad was rescued.

In my dad's case he was able to attend dental school in the Midwest, even though he had to start over. This was only made possible by being advocated for by Professor Beale. Dad did ask for help from his former mission school in Los Angeles, a Maryknoll mission school, and the priest there was able to help him out with some money for tuition. That also explains why my dad never missed donating to Maryknoll's mission school for many many years afterwards. The point for including this story is that without this intervention and advocacy in my father's adult education, I would more than likely not be here. My dad after graduation was then drafted into the military, the same military that denied him his liberty years earlier. But because of the advocacy that he experienced and the attitude of gratitude that he exhibited throughout his early life, dad continued to lead an extraordinarily productive life and continues to be an extraordinary human being at 96. (He made his 97th birthday and passed away on April 8 of this year.) It is interesting that the technology of that time (1942-1943) were not yet on the level of personal computers of today. The most that was being used were slide rulers and abacuses. My dad's inclusion at this point has to do with what is considered the period between 1931-1946 where my dad remembered at 13 years old, cranking up the Model A Ford and driving his father around because my dad, not his father, had the technical grasp of that technology. My dad, Henry Ema, just passed after the completion of this paper but the legacy of his advocacy and his model of service is what has guided me and countless others that he came in contact with. We will miss you Dad.

BEGINNING PERSONAL EDUCATION AS WELL AS TEACHING EXPERIENCE

During my earlier years in school, I attended Catholic School, recalling that my own instruction and learning was geared to the concept of "learning by assignment", which was learning by pedagogical techniques and sometimes by rote memory. I didn't identify those techniques as pedagogical until I found out later that is what they were called but did not know what they were called at the time. Much later, as I began teaching and learning through and about adult learning techniques using andragogy but not really identified as andragogy. I later identified that many of the ways that I taught best were ways that I had been following much of the Andragogical methods for much of my own early career. I found that during my early teaching in the late 70 and early 80s, I taught in parochial or religious schools setting usually six out of seven periods a day to a very specific and very different group of students. In a lot of ways I was teaching 6 six different preps each day. Much of the teaching came directly from the content of books because that is the way the curriculum was assembled. There was a very specific sequence that needed to be followed and what made the situation much more intolerable was the lack of professional development and administrative support. Later I taught in a private school teaching chemistry and some physical science classes in that school. I was teaching again five or six classes a day following a book and again following a closely orchestrated curriculum that was tying content to book sequence for simplicity and uniformity. Later in 1985, I began teaching in an Illinois junior/community college for the next 10 years, I taught part time mainly in night school and learned early on that I was teaching in a different venue because I was teaching students in the age range of young adults (17-20s) through 80 years old. Although I did not understand the concept of adult education in a formal sense, what I did understand was that how and what I taught content wise was not as important as the rapport that I established with my students. Much of what I began to understand as adult education was also part of a shared definition with the term advocacy. In many ways the logical step was to link Advocacy with Andragogy since much of the concepts of each tended to overlap.

PERSONAL BACKGROUND HISTORY: A BEGINNING OF TECHNOLOGY AND UNDERSTANDING

I began by recalling my first job with the Boy Scouts at a Boy Scout summer camp when I was 16 and realized that my first teaching assignment was working with other scouts and helping them use preexisting booklets about Boy Scout subject matter. The technology of that time period consisted of very readable pamphlets and brochures. These pamphlets or booklets were self-contained modular courses. Each booklet had reasonable content expectations and specific guidelines. In addition each booklet's content taught and helped the student learn a limited topic area with enough expertise to compile a reasonable model or portfolio. These booklets allowed scouts (students who were members of the organization) to meet the guidelines of the subject being taught. More specifically, the booklets might better be described as a "natural science and other content specific merit badge" modules with very narrowly designed content related to outdoors, nature, environment and camping related topic areas. The way that the merit badge system was set up is to allow personal self-directed and completely self-paced personal study of a particular subject matter for eventual testing or portfolio display as a project. The purpose of this display or presentation is to show that the students (other Boy Scout members) have read the background information in the packet and have satisfied the self-directed self-paced teaching packets. I realized early on that the packets were interesting to motivated individuals and were in themselves self-directed tools for teaching a particular subject area. For that period of time 1960-1973, although other technologies were beginning to emerge, these pamphlets were the state of the art teaching tool and the highest in technologically advanced teaching materials available as personal copies that were the most readily accessible that these scouts (students) could use. Analyzing this Boy Scout packet series further I realized that the course was set up to provide the student, a self-contained, self-paced and self-directed set of course work. Each packet or module was a complete study packet with an evaluation piece attached to it. Once completed the instructor can evaluate the work of the student with the packet and awards the merit badge (pass or fail) and may suggest other activities and additional content specific merit badge work that the student can pursue to obtain more merit badges. This external motivation, the award of the merit badge, appeared to be a huge motivational factor for the students (Boy Scouts) that allowed them to obtain merit badges and gain more knowledge based on digestible content laden modules. This appeared to me to be even further evidence to advance the concept of andragogy since, in part, these students are motivated to complete their assignment and collect their grades (their merit badges) or credit that builds on past learning and knowledge anchors that helps them to complete additional content based course work. (Knowles)

MY EDUCATIONAL BACKGROUND

Later in my own undergraduate education 1974, I needed a course to complete a particular sequence in my education. I had to find one that was compatible to the department's curriculum requirements. I found the course and got approval and then found myself taking a course that was self-directed and self-paced for summer credit at the local community college branch near my home. While taking this class, even though it was not an everyday class meeting, it was my first non-in-residence class, Not to dissimilar to just studying in the library, I was on my own and was given my own summer packet or modules that once completed, provided the credit needed by my program for me to finish and complete the science requirement. It was my first exposure to a hybrid or modified distance learning model. It was a form of independent study that was guided by the packet. Once completed, I would be asked to come in to the college and take an exam to receive credit. I was not required to come to any classes (all materials were self-contained) but was required to finish the packets at my own pace within a reasonable time period. The Andragogical piece (adult education part of self-motivation) is that I had to be motivated to complete the package much as the booklets for Boy Scouts merit badges had to be completed by motivation and self -determination. No one would be pushing us to finish except ourselves and our own motivational force. We would use the educational technology of the time. Again it was not computing technology since personal computing technology was yet immature. It was not a simple transition for teaching and learning as this was not an area of consistency yet. Few systems were even close in architecture and many operating systems were proprietary. During my class time in 1974–1975 the personal computers were still a buzz and not a reality for real home use yet. So the technology of my time was still the pamphlets or modules. Fortunately these booklets included everything that a person would need or want to know to answer very specific questions or complete a course of study. With the help of my dad I was able to purchase my first Apple II for a whopping 2000.00 and my dad had to cosign for it. I do remember my brother paying over a 100.00 for a Texas Instrument calculator that only did addition, subtraction, multiplication and division. I don't think that it did much of anything else. I know he was really mad at the price a few years down the line. That same 100.00 could buy a whole lot more.

MY EARLY WORK EXPOSURE TO ADVOCACY: LINK TO ADULT EDUCATION

I was an adjunct instructor for the business department/data processing division at the Community College in Southwestern Illinois, 1985-1995, there was a huge difference between types of technology systems in each location that I had class in. My own training was on huge computer mainframes of the time. It was my first exposure and learning experience programming using key punch cards with individual line programming. In my own class work, in order to get our work done for class, we had to literally rush to the computer input device in the basement of the university building that we had class, ran to the punch card machine to get the punch cards, and then load the card readers, and hope that our loaded programs would work correctly the first time. The first one to let it run and create the program product that we needed to turn in the next class day, was definitely a happy person. There was only ONE input device, so yes we literally ran to the basement to get in line to punch in our data and get our cards read. It was a far cry from the personal computer that each district was in the process of getting for their student and night school classes. This was only a few years later as personal computers were becoming more available and affordable. In these classes as the instructor, I needed to create a learning environment for each place that I was holding class and for each of the students so that it was comfortable for them to learn data processing, programming, and other computer related information. When I started there in 1985 no two sites in any of the extension centers had the same type of computers in any of the labs. It was not readily noticeable but what made each of the locations interesting is that the unrelated systems actually did have a common thread for each of the systems on their campus. That common piece was the fact that all the systems used some form of simple of basic programming language. The educators and administrators made certain that the systems that were put into place for each campus extension center was at least able to use some basic programming language or apple equivalent. What I noticed about each of the student groups/classes in each situation, was that these computer systems though very different, they were able to provide the minimal resources necessary to hold class. As an instructor we had to be able to learn and conform or at least adapt to the systems that we were being exposed and our students needed. The site centers administrators had the ability to lease or buy computer systems or equipment in the extension centers necessary to keep the labs running. Unfortunately many of the centers had systems that were very different from what many of the students, regardless of the type of computer that these students were used to using, had at home. It was important that the students were given the resources that they were going to need to be successful in this class. The interesting part is that the instructor myself, had to advocated for each of the extension centers classes that I taught. I had to create the unique learning environment for each class. Each group or class had to conform to the system that they would be using but with my cleaver trickery, resourcefulness or my expertise in using different systems, it was easy for me to make the systems work for the students and conform to where their home location. I also tried to make what they learned transportable to their home use. As and educational system this was quite a different system for me to teach in since I was used to teaching middle school through 12 mainly high schools. Junior College taught me a different form of teaching, a different method of instruction in the sense that most if not all of my students in the class were at least 18 years or older. Because of that I later learned that the term that is used in adult education is not pedagogy but andragogy. The interesting part about andragogy or adult education as it's sometimes referred to, is that the adult learners are usually more motivated to learn and has a purpose and a reason why they are taking a class. Because they have a different set of motivating factors, these particular students have a different reason and a different incentive to keep learning. The learner centered approach works extremely well with these students. And the amazing thing about teaching is that the adult learner can be the epitome of what a goal centered, learner centered students should be. Sometimes it is because the adult learner are so motivated that they are not concerned with issues in the classroom so much as the subject content of the class. They are motivated to know the subject matter and will question the status quo versus in pedagogy sometimes the student will just accept what the instructor says without challenge. This form of blind obedience is sometimes a problem for adult education. The blind obedience that some instructors require in a particular subject, doesn't necessarily lend itself well to the learner and in some circles could be viewed as bullying or some other form of oppression. Many learners require their instructors to be an advocate for them and to be someone that will create the environment for them to learn. Because it was necessary for me to change the environment of the students in my class to meet their needs in a lot of ways I learned what it really bad to be an advocate for my students. Many times I had to go to those in charge of the night school and ask for materials supplies and other things that should have been provided to the students through the system and the materials available to for the class. The interesting part about being an advocate for my students really was a more common sense approach. As an adult myself I knew what I would need to have this school provide or what needs to be changed in order to make the environment and the subject matter even more user friendly or learner centered as the current term is being used. But in a lot of cases, the term user friendly can be transformed into learner centered to describe what I would try to do to change the environment in my room for my class.

MY ADVOCACY HISTORY

My own journey as an advocate became clear when I started teaching at a public school in the F F school district and joined the building union. When I was asked to help with the negotiation of benefits and pay, I didn't have to be asked twice. What I learned was not just the training side of negotiation but also the side of understanding andragogy and adult learning theory in a practical application arena. Training came in the form of professional development for leaders and for teacher facilitators; and for the first time I learned what it was like to be valued and listened to. As an adult learner I was motivated because I was going to be thrust into the arena of negotiations with administrators and teachers and I was being put into the center as the leader. I am a fast learner but I also realized very quickly that beyond skills I also needed to establish a level of rapport. Being truthful and honest in my dealings with the administrators and pushing for the needs of the students and educators in my district, the level of rapport needed was important on all levels for the negotiations to be successful. This training by fire taught me the value of rapport in the classroom and taught me the value of listening to my students while trying to meet their educational needs and goals and providing the catalyst for real growth and learning. Tapping into the rapport of the class helped to reach the educational motivation that I needed to get my content across and help the students to really learn day to day, week to week.

My training started early on many, many years ago but my formal advocacy training started with my union and their teacher leaders / facilitators / trainers first showing me assertiveness and the power of language modules and the module of leadership and organization. Slowly many years later I also was trained as a trainer / presenter in social justice and cultural competency. Starting initially in 1999 and going on continuing to the present the training in my union has not ended and will not any time soon. What has happened is a resurgence of the training and the modules that are being offered to union locals in school districts across the country and around the world. There are many locals with members that need to be trained and taught and molded to become advocates to for their own members and students. The training follows adult learning modalities that are taught by educator trainers who volunteer and they themselves are motivated to pass on their training to other educators. These same trainers in turn have been taught by professional adult educators using the latest training techniques and training research.

ADVOCACY DEFINED AND LINKED TO EDUCATIONAL RESOURCES

Advocacy by definition is "an act or process of supporting a cause or proposal, or an act of advocating for something" at least according to Merriam-Webster online. Andragogy is "1. The science of understanding (=theory) and supporting (=practice) lifelong and life-wide education of adults. 2. In the tradition of Malcolm Knowles, andragogy is a specific theoretical and practical approach based on a humanistic conception of self-directed and autonomous learners and teachers as facilitators of learning." The overlap that I perceived was that adult educators were advocates for their students creating the environment that can help them with their understanding and learning and lifelong learning goals. As adult educators, facilitators and coaches, these instructors have a daunting task because it is sometimes difficult to separate their role of advocate from their role of instructor in an adult education setting. Motivation is a key difference between what defines andragogy from pedagogy and probably shapes the concepts that drive individual adult learning versus the training and education of that of a child. Each Adults acts as their own advocate by representing themselves in their own education but seeking the right fit for their own lifelong learning goals.

MY EDUCATIONAL LINK AND ASSESSMENT OF LEARNING

What I learned at that time in those different areas of education was the term advocacy, even though I didn't really understand the term at first. What I did found out, and later discovered, was that as an instructor, facilitator, coach or traditional teacher what I had to do was be more than the content person with the ability to adjust to the needs of my students. I would become the filter or the conduit for learning for the students and I needed to adjust my style and what I presented that was conducive to learning and the learning environment or community that I was trying to create for my student no matter what age and no matter what subject area.

What I also learned was that through advocacy and establishing rapport with my students, I could really grasp a better understanding of the student's needs. In this way I was able to better communicate the subject matter with your students, audience or participants and then through active listening and more intently focusing on the students, I was able to better understand their needs and their wants. This also allowed me to better discern what advocacy really means and how to best serve these students. It also allowed me to search for what background information do I have that will help me look for the common definitions and meanings and also to look for background data in the literature.

OBSERVATION AND FUTURE STUDIES AND OPINIONS ABOUT THE INCIDENT IN RECENT NEWS

As the issues of many American cities and the unrest that has followed and other incidents that have unfolded in the last few months, I realized that what we have been doing in the classroom in the last few years before I retired and what I have been teaching and advocating to adult learners, instructors and teacher leaders and educators across the country is the same message that I have successfully used in the classroom for almost 35 years. All of the students both in their teens and into their nineties have all been taught the use of the inquiry method and adult learning strategies by myself and my colleagues for at least the last fifteen years. The ideas of student centered and adult learning theory go hand and hand with advocacy since no matter what area we are in and what venue we have been teaching in, all of these learners are converting or need to at least acknowledge that learning is life long and that advocating for our students and their environment is part of our job and not just an adjunct. Mixed with these is the concept of social justice and cultural competence due to the lack of equity in many of our communities. Our communities are the real winners rather than losers if our community can be sustained and allowed to grow and thrive. Ferguson is not a community that is dying but is a community that is necessary to allow continuing on their own course. They had been a community that came together for their students and fought for their students and education. Many of their students grew up, became educated and came back to the community and helped to make their community a better place to live. Education of the community infrastructure, the administrators and law enforcement, is also necessary and less emphasis on the "old school " approach to law enforcement and back to the community building activity that has been the attitude of many of the past leaders of that community. They understood their community and their own people and their own unique culture and accepted the aberrant nature of some in the community that chose to be disruptive. They policed their own and in the past created a community. In recent years, that has changed dramatically with less emphasis on the understanding of the community and more assimilation mentality that that is not the way that our society should be acting. May be it is that more recent attitude that needs to be looked at and discarded. Education of the "new administrators" needs to be considered and maybe implemented. The attitude that education is just for "kids and the young adults" should be rethought. Lifelong learning leads to communal understanding and commitment to culture and growth. Listening to your community causes real change and growth to occur. Establishing rapport and community with your work environment makes the environment for growth happen.

ACKNOWLEDGEMENTS

National Education Association, Missouri National Education Association, F F Education Association, F F School District,

REFERENCES

[1] Granger, C.R.: 1996, *The Naturalistic Education Theory: In Search of a Unified Learning Theory for Instructional Methodology and Tactical Education*, Journal of Thought 31(2), 85-96.

[2] Henschke, J. A. (1998). *Historical antecedents shaping concepts of andragogy: A comparison of sources and roots.* Proceedings of the Third International Conference on Research in Comparative Andragogy. Bled, Radlovjica, Slovenia.

[3] Isaac, E. P. (2011). *Barriers to adult education participation, distance education, and learning.* In V. C. X. Wang (Ed.), Encyclopedia of information communication technologies and adult education integration (pp. 1100-1112). Charlotte, NC: Information Age Publishing. , CA: Sage.

[4] Knowles, M. (1980). *The modern practice of adult education.* New York: Association Press, & Cambridge Book Publishers.

[5] Knowles, M. (1984). *The adult learner: A neglected species.* Houston: Gulf Publishing.

[6] Wilmarth, P. J. (2010) *Comparative Perceptions of Adult learners in an Online and Face-to-Face Course*, Dissertation presented to University of Missouri Saint Louis (UMSL)

[7] Washington, B. T. and Dubois, W

An Alternative Approach to Prior Learning and Advanced Placement in Post-Secondary Programs for Veterans: The Canadian Experience

K.J. Wainwright, Amy Fell, Sonia Dhaliwal
BC Institute of Technology

OVERVIEW

In 2006 British Columbia Institute of Technology (BCIT) partnered with Honor House, a group of business leaders, veterans and Canadian forces members supporting wounded soldiers returning from the Afghanistan mission to provide career counseling and resume writing services. It quickly became apparent through BCIT's work with Afghanistan veterans that there was a significant amount of military training and experience that potentially matched high skill demands in the labor market and therefore learning outcomes at post-secondary institutions. In 2006, Canadian post-secondary institutions offered limited transfer credit for military training. Based on experience acquired through the partnership with Honor House, BCIT established a student research project with the purpose to study the possibility of expanding recognition of military training based on an assumption that the combination of military training and experience could reveal potential credit equivalencies that were not currently articulated.

The potential for establishing advanced placement education pathways for soldiers in post-secondary programs posed two challenges. The first was the nature of the military training model did not lend itself well to traditional prior learning assessment processes. The second challenge, or question, was whether any systematic patterns existed that would allow us to identify common skills, traits and abilities within a cohort, thereby allowing economies of scale and other efficiency gains in the assessment and review process.

In addition to the logistical challenges mentioned above, research identified the issue of veteran "engagement" as one of the major challenges in developing successful pathways and advanced placement programs to support transition. Many countries offering education programs to assist veterans in transitioning to civilian life – including Canada and the United States – had experienced the problem of engagement on the part of veterans. Research identified that veteran engagement was the result of two main barriers. First, the change in environment from military life to civilian life was perceived as too vast. Second, existing prior learning program articulations available to veterans were aligned with their military experience rather than their post-secondary training interests. Therefore, to enable veterans' transition through post-secondary education pathways veterans required holistic support through the transition period and post-secondary program options focused on veterans' interests and preferences.

In 2009 BCIT launched its Military Skills Conversion Program.[1] While the program's primary purpose was to build and offer educational pathways, a holistic approach was adopted which included a comprehensive group of services including resume writing and job search skills, entrepreneurial workshops for veterans and a network of support services and referrals to agencies specializing in transition support. BCIT partnered with other organizations including the Veterans Transition Program (which treated PTSD) and the Royal Canadian Legion. The program started as a pilot project and has grown into the single largest program of its kind in the Canadian post-secondary system. Currently there are 42 soldiers enrolled in the various BCIT programs and 41 have graduated since the launch of the project. The GPA's of the soldiers who have graduated are higher than their civilian counterparts on average. Ninety-five percent of the graduates have GPA's higher than 70% with half of these being honors students with GPA's over 80%.

---

[1] The program was initially launched under the name "The Reservist Re-Entry Program", which was, in part' due to the large number of reserve regiments in the local community. The name was later changed to reflect the program's broader appeal to all service men and women, regardless of status (regular, reserve, veteran).

THE PILOT PROJECT AT BCIT

The BC Institute of Technology has an enrollment of 46,000 full and part-time students. It has 340 programs that range from certificate to master degrees. The scope of its programming includes trades, engineering diplomas and degrees, a variety of health science diplomas and a nursing degree, as well as one of the largest business schools in the province that offers over 20 different diplomas and two bachelor degrees.

A feature of the BCIT model that is significant to this project is the cohort-based delivery model of full-time programs. Full-time diploma program students are admitted into a program and assigned to a cohort. Students in a cohort are registered in the same courses and are assigned the same curriculum, workload and schedule. With very few exceptions to the model, all students progress through the program in the courses at the same pace. Except for attrition, all students within a cohort begin and graduate from a program at the same time. This feature of the BCIT education model offers two benefits in this context. First, the cohort model of program delivery mirrors aspects of the military environment. Second, it enables the ability to track and test groups of students over time that will have the same incremental education at every instance of testing. The lack of variability in course load and program progression produces a "clean" data set.

ARTICULATING MILITARY TRAINING – OVERCOMING PERCEIVED SYSTEMATIC LIMITATIONS

Pedagogical conventions dictate a prescribed method for assessing prior learning and establishing post-secondary learning outcome equivalencies through what is commonly known as Prior Learning Assessment and Recognition (PLAR). Military training utilizes the combination of training and experience to train soldiers, which posed a challenge in assessing prior learning equivalencies due to conventional thinking regarding achievement of a learning outcome. In order to fairly consider the breadth and depth of the many disciplines associated with military training a new method of prior learning assessment was required. It also became apparent that given the military training model, the prior learning assessment could be grouped and "systematized". Creating an approach that enabled systematized prior learning assessment (PLAR) would significantly reduce the labor-intensive resources necessary for individual assessment, which had historically served as a barrier to assessment for many post-secondary institutes. This evolved an approach to PLAR called Advanced Placement and Prior Learning (APPL) that arose from a 2009 pilot project at BCIT.

One significant difference about this pilot project was the systematized approach used to determine program admission. Normally admission is determined through completion of primary academic requirements, in this case Grade 12 English and Grade 11 Math, and an assessment of prior post-secondary academic work: grades in courses and credentials previously earned by the applicant. For soldiers, we developed an outcomes based approach that aimed to compare military training and experience outcomes with post-secondary program completion outcomes.

Generating Program Completion Outcomes

To start, we identified program completion outcomes: the necessary skills and abilities required for successful completion of a program. Essentially, we asked the question *"If we replicated the total amount of training and development embodied in the soldiers being assessed, what would such a program look like in the BCIT framework and what level of credential would be awarded for such a program?"*

To address the problem of determining equivalencies, an alternative assessment model was developed. Using Applied Placement and Prior Learning (APPL), the new assessment model, a block learning outcome approach was created. First, a cross-section of diploma programs were reviewed, breaking down individual courses into learning outcomes. This resulted in a set of learning outcomes for each program. Second, a scorecard system was developed that allowed an individual to be scored as to the relative proficiency of each learning outcome. The scorecard created a method to assess both the breadth and depth of learning outcomes. The scorecard generated an overall program benchmark based on learning outcome proficiency rather than credits earned or grade point average. In a similar fashion, all of the basic training models for the Canadian Forces (army branch) were also assessed. This produced a common metric for comparison of military training to BCIT programs.

Generating Military History Completion Outcomes

Review and comparison of military training and work history proved complex and challenging. The learning outcomes for the military programs were compared, both individually and as a block, to the diploma program outcomes. While there were great deals of differences in many of the technical, field specific outcomes, there was a high degree of overlap in many of the general learning outcomes (i.e. teamwork, problem solving, time management, etc.)

An extensive mapping process was created to capture and analyze learning outcomes acquired through military training modules and link them to learning outcomes and courses at BCIT. The mapping process was carried out in collaboration with the training officers and commanding officers of local regiments to develop a skills inventory. In addition to the evaluation and mapping of the military training modules, extensive research was done to reveal potential learning outcomes associated with deployment and the experience of soldiers during the deployment period. The mapping process established standardized profiles on duties, expectations, and experiences of deployment.[2]

The evaluation tools consisted of a combination of aptitude and problem solving tests, personality profiles, and interviews that reviewed each soldier's military and work history. A review of military training and work history included assessment of a soldier's military training module completion, deployment and military service experience. The evaluation tools created a standardized approach to assessing military training modules and experience against the established program completion outcomes.

---

[2] The majority of applicants had deployed to Afghanistan, however the program also had applicants who had been part of earlier missions including Bosnia and Somalia.

FINDINGS

The initial research revealed two interesting findings. First, the assessed skills and abilities of the soldiers far exceeded the expected outcomes of military training modules. Second, a soldier's military history was not indicative of his or her interests and aptitudes. This supports proposition that an outcomes based assessment approach is a more appropriate method of evaluation. Analysis of soldiers showed that those who deployed, or were eligible to deploy, had received the same minimum amount of standardized training. This translated to a high degree of consistency across modules being mapped into post-secondary programs. Further, it was determined that the pre-deployment level of training was equivalent to a technical diploma.[3]

Interest and Aptitude-Lens vs Reality

The pilot project employed the World of Work Inventory (WOWI[4]) to determine aptitude and interests of project participants. WOWI results indicated strong interest and fit for areas of business, public services, and health sciences. In contrast, a credential based evaluation considering only formal military modules as transcripts would likely have revealed that the best post-secondary fit would be found in trades training or vocational program such as mechanics, truck-driving, or construction. The soldiers themselves, in self-evaluation reports, indicated that they felt they had been best prepared for policing or private security careers because they hold the perception that their training is position specific. Given the educational requirements of most Canadian police forces, most soldiers believed private security or laborer were the most likely career paths available.

A BCIT Program Fit

---

[3] The definition of a technical diploma used here is a two-year, full-time diploma in either vocational or academic fields which is focused in scope.

[4] WOWI, or World of Work Inventory, is an assessment tool that measures both aptitudes and interests of individual. WOWI benchmarks the individual against two criteria: a) relative to others of the same age; and b) relative to others of the same education level. WOWI has proven successful in matching individuals to professions where they will experience a high level of satisfaction.

The WOWI results, combined with results of the learning outcomes scorecard and interview process, led to the conclusion that a majority of the soldiers had both the ability and suitability to be successful as advanced placement students in business diploma programs or as direct entry to the advanced diploma, which delivers the foundation courses for entry to the degree completion program in business administration. BCIT programming tends to be modular in nature, where diplomas can ladder into advanced diplomas and degree completion programs.[5]

BENCHMARKING THE MODEL

In order to validate the findings in the pilot and determine potential growth of the program into other fields, extensive benchmarking was carried out by testing and evaluating the civilian counterparts in the business management diploma program. Benchmarking involved several elements; including a) application of World of Work Inventory, b) statistical analysis of course grades and GPA's, c) attrition ratios, and d) peer and faculty feedback. The data came from test scores, questionnaires, and focus groups.

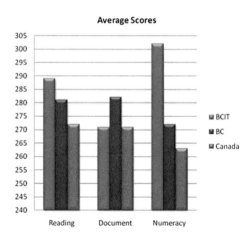

In addition to the evaluations above, the students in the business program, both civilian and military, are part of a time series study using the "Test of

---

[5] At BCIT many fields of study are structured in a framework known as the "2 by 2 model". A two year diploma ladders into a 60 credit degree completion program.

Work Place Essential Skills" (TOWES[6]) testing tool. First, the TOWES was issued to students at regular intervals through their academic progression to measure the development of their workplace skills. The purpose was to measure the extent students acquired or developed relevant human capital in the context of TOWES. Second, the TOWES was used as a cross-sectional study of soldiers and civilians in the business program. The TOWES was used both to benchmark soldiers and civilians at the initial admissions stage and as a metric to evaluate relative progression over the life of the program.

TOWES AND BCIT BUSINESS STUDENTS

The application of the TOWES test on business students at BCIT produced the following: First, BCIT students, on average, scored higher than the HRDC findings for the BC population and the Canadian population in all three categories. Second, students who completed two years of the business program scored higher than the students tested at the end of one year in all three categories. There was a significant rise in scores in reading and numeracy in comparison to the first and second year students. While the first year students were strong in document use relative to numeracy and reading, there is a significant upward shift in the score between first and second year students in this area as well. While the sample was limited to students in business programs, the results suggest that students at BCIT see a marked improvement in their essential workplace skills.

BCIT AND RESERVISTS

After analyzing the results from the Canadian reservists and comparing them to the Business students at BCIT, we found that, on average, reservists scores were between those of first year and second year students. Based on an

---

[6] In the early 1990s, the Government of Canada launched the Essential Skills Research Project (ESRP). The Project identified nine Essential Skills: reading text, document use, numeracy, writing, oral communication, working with others, thinking skills, computer use, and continuous learning. The ESRP developed a way to profile the skill requirements of occupations in the labour market which lead to the development of TOWES. The TOWES allows employers to test their workers to determine their levels of those Essential Skills and put into place plans for improving them to achieve better productivity and workplace safety.

essential skills evaluation, reservists entered the program with higher skills scores than their civilian counterparts. These results are consistent with the overall performance of reservists in the pilot program. WOWI results revealed that Canadian reservists were not significantly different from the students in vocational training potential, job satisfaction indicators and career interest activities.

The next issue to be addressed was to determine if there were common characteristics, skills, and abilities within the soldiers as a group. Further, it was necessary to evaluate these attributes in a manner that allowed direct comparisons to civilian activities, in particular students in post-secondary programs. This was done using focus groups, extensive one-on-one interviews and standardized testing with exams such as Test of Workplace Essential Skills (TOWES) and World of Work Inventory (WOWI). The findings of the empirical research demonstrated a high degree of homogeneity across the reservists in the sample. Further, when compared to post-secondary students who had also participated in the same testing procedure, the reservists scored higher than students who had completed one year of post-secondary education and were slightly below the average scores of students who had completed technical diplomas.

As a result of the findings, reservists were given advanced placement into a program that normally required a minimum of a diploma as a prerequisite. The initial results of the pilot program proved successful. As of June 2012, 90% of the reservists at BCIT completed the program. Further, the average GPA of the reservists was higher than the overall program GPA. Seventy-five percent of the soldiers who graduated from the diploma program went on to complete their bachelor's degree within 12 to 18 months.

The success of the pilot project with the reservists suggested that the model could be expanded and applied to other groups such as first responders and groups of mature students with common characteristics, as well as those from population groups identified as having common characteristics and experiences (i.e. remote communities and Aboriginals).

ENGAGEMENT

Focus groups and interviews were used to address two issues. The first was to validate the findings of the prior learning assessments and TOWES scores by reviewing each participant's history and records. The second purpose of the focus group and interview process was to address the problem of "engagement." Experience from the pilot program with the reservists reinforced the findings of researchers[7] regarding the problem of certain groups not engaging in educational opportunities, even when fully funded.

The focus groups revealed that veterans believed their training prepared them for military service; however, they had not considered potential similarities and synergies between military training and post-secondary education or civilian careers. Veterans often reported a sense of uncertainty at the prospect of transitioning from their environment into the culture of a typical post-secondary institute. In other instances, veterans were unaware of the value of the skills and abilities they possessed and therefore struggled to believe they were equipped for programs they qualified for. Given the nature of military training, veterans have the perception that their training is only specific to their position in the military.

EXPANSION OF THE MODEL: THE FUTURE OF ADVANCED PLACEMENT AND PRIOR LEARNING (APPL)

Expansion of the APPL Model requires ongoing research and support. Research has indicated that expanding the breadth of pathways available to veterans and expanding the availability of APPL pathways in post-secondary institutions across Canada is required to address engagement issues.

Ongoing research will continue the development of the APPL assessment model to reveal the value of military training and experience in the context of post-secondary learning outcomes across program offerings. At present, veterans have access to advanced placement into 13 BCIT programs ranging

---

[7] Eliott, Marta; Gonzalez, Carlene; and Larsen, Barbara. "U.S. Military Veterans Transition to College: Combat, PTSD, and Alienation on Campus", (2011) Journal of Student Affairs Research and Practice, Vol 48, Issue 3

from business, telecommunications, forensics, construction, and engineering. The goal is to continue to map advanced placement pathways into health sciences, electrical, mechanical and civil engineering programs.

Expanding access across Canada requires the creation of several partnerships and sponsorship. In 2012 the model was presented to the Canadian Senate[8], which generated significant interest in the development of a national program. The Federal Government, including Veteran Affairs Canada, Employment and Social Development Canada, and National Defense and the Canadian Armed Forces currently supports the Military Skills Conversion Program. In 2014, a national consortium convened by Canada Company[9], part of Military Employment Transition (MET) was established to pursue expansion of APPL in post-secondary institutions across Canada. BCIT leads the national consortium with the goal to build a network of post-secondary institutions that grant credits for military training, to address education and employment barriers and increase mobility of soldiers.

BIBLIOGRAPHY

Journals

[1] Campbell, B., Coff, R., & Kryscynski, D. (2012, July). Rethinking Sustained Competitive Advantage from Human Capital. *Academy of Management Review*, 37(3), 376-395.

[2] Foster, K., Neidert, G. B.-R., Artaleio, D., & Caruso, D. (2010, November). A psychological profile of surgeons and surgical residents. Journal of Surgical Education, 67, 359-70.

[3] Jepson, C., & Montgomer, M. (2012, February). Back to School: An application of human capital theory for mature workers. Economics of Education Review, 31(1), 168-178.

---

[8] The Canadian Senate had been tasked with doing a complete review of the state of veterans in Canada, including all programs, support services to aid in transition to civilian life.

[9] Canada Company is a not-for-profit national organization supported by Veteran Affairs. Canada Company has a mandate to transition veterans into civilian careers and works with organizations, such "Helmets to Hardhats" and the "10,000 Job Initiative"

[4] Ndingury, E., Prieto, L., & Machtmes, K. (2012, June). Human Capital Development Dynamics: The Knowledge Based Approach. Academy of Strategic Management Journal, 11(2), 121-136.

[5] Tatoglu, F. Y. (2012). The Relationships between Human Capital Investment and Economic Growth: A Panel Error Correction Model. Journal of Economic and Social Research, 13(2), 75-88.

[6] Whiting, H., & Kline, T. J. (2006, December). Assessment of the equivalence of conventional versus computer administration of the Test of Workplace Essential Skills. International Journal of Training and Development, 10(4), 285-290.

Government

[7] Government of Ontario. (2012, 01 30). What do Canadian employers want? Retrieved from settlement.org: http://settlement.org/sys/faqs_detail.asp?k=WORK_CUL&faq_id=4001128

[8] Human Resources and Skills Development Canada. (2012, 06 16). Learning - Educational Attainment. Retrieved from hrsdc.gc.ca: http://www4.hrsdc.gc.ca/.3ndic.1t.4r@-eng.jsp?iid=29

[9] Statistics Canada. (2008). Trends in the Age Composition of College and University Students and Graduates. Retrieved from statscan.gc.ca: http://www.statcan.gc.ca/pub/81-004-x/2010005/article/11386-eng.htm

[10] Statistics Canada. (2008, 12 01). Why are the majority of university students women? Retrieved from statcan.gc.ca: http://www.statcan.gc.ca/pub/81-004-x/2008001/article/10561-eng.htm

[11] Statistics Canada. (2011). Postsecondary Education Participation among Underrepresented and Minority Groups. Retrieved 06 16, 2012, from http://www.statcan.gc.ca/pub/81-004-x/2011004/article/11595-eng.htm#a

[12] ORGANIZATIONAL, SOCIAL AND DEMOGRAPHIC CHANGE IN THE CANADIAN FORCES Source: http://www.internationalmta.org/1998/9837.html

[13] Statistics Canada July 2008 Perspectives – A Profile on Canadian Forces by Jungwee Park Source: http://www.statcan.gc.ca/pub/75-001-x/2008107/pdf/10657-eng.pdf

[14] Canadian forces deployed outside of Canada 1992-2003 Government of Canada Source: http://www.army.forces.gc.ca/land-terre/life-vie/army-armee/statistics-statistiques-eng.asp Date Modified: 2009-07-27

[15] Fit to Serve: Universality of Service and Related Support Programs June 29, 2010 Source: http://www.forces.gc.ca/site/news-nouvelles/news-nouvelles-eng.asp?cat=03&id=3449

Canadian Forces

[16] ARMY DP 1 – INFANTRYMAN Training Plan A-P9-031-DP1/PH-B01 November 2007 Source: Canadian Forces, Seaforth Highlanders, Regimental Headquarters: Seaforth Armoury 1650 Burrard Street Vancouver, BC V6j 3G4

[17] ARMY NCM DP 1 BASIC MILITARY QUALIFICATION A-PD-050-BMQ/PH-H16 November 2007 Source: Canadian Forces, Seaforth Highlanders, Regimental Headquarters: Seaforth Armoury 1650 Burrard Street Vancouver, BC V6j 3G4

[18] ARMY NCM DP 1 – SOLDIER QUALIFICATION A-P2-002-D10/PH-B01 September 2004 Source: Canadian Forces, Seaforth Highlanders, Regimental Headquarters: Seaforth Armoury 1650 Burrard Street Vancouver, BC V6j 3G4

[19] DP 2 ARMOUR RECONNAISSANCE OBSERVER A-P2-011-S01/PH-B01 May 2005 Source: Canadian Forces, Seaforth Highlanders, Regimental Headquarters: Seaforth Armoury 1650 Burrard Street Vancouver, BC V6j 3G4

[20] MOC NCM DP2 INFANTRY PLATOON SUPPORT WEAPONS A-P9-031-DP2/PH-B01 November 2005 Source: Canadian Forces, Seaforth Highlanders, Regimental Headquarters: Seaforth Armoury 1650 Burrard Street Vancouver, BC V6j 3G4

[21] TACTICAL COMBAT CASUALTY CARE April 2006 Source: Canadian Forces, Seaforth Highlanders, Regimental Headquarters: Seaforth Armoury 1650 Burrard Street Vancouver, BC V6j 3G4

Other (magazines, blogs, program websites)

[22] Allevne, S. (2012, February). Getting a Head Start. Black Enterprise, 42(7), p. 48.

[23] Association of Canadian Community Colleges. 11 October 2012 <http://www.accc.ca/xp/index.php/en/advocacy/advskills-actplan>.

[24] Bailey, P. D. (2011, 11 27). The Role of Class Difficulty in College Grade Point Averages. Retrieved from econweb.umd.edu: http://econweb.umd.edu/~bailey/Paul_Bailey_JMPaper.pdf

[25] Canadian Council on Learning. (2010). What is the future of learning in Canada? Retrieved from www.ccl-cca.ca: http://www.ccl-cca.ca/pdfs/CEOCorner/2010-10-11WhatistheFutureofLearninginCanada.pdf

[26] Canadian Federation of Independent Business. (2009, 05). Canada's Training Ground. Retrieved from www.cfib-fcei.ca: http://www.cfib-fcei.ca/english/article/368-canada-s-training-ground.html

[27] Canadian Policy Research Networks. (2006). Employer Investment in Workplace Learning in Canada. Retrieved from www.ccl-cca.ca: http://www.ccl-cca.ca/pdfs/WLKC/EmployerInvestmentWorkplaceLearningCCLCPRN.pdf

[28] Canadian Policy Research Networks. (2009, 02 27). Enhancing Access to Post-Secondary Education in Canada: An Exploration of Early Intervention Initiatives in Selected Countries. Retrieved from www.cprn.org: http://www.cprn.org/documents/51117_EN.pdf

[29] Carey, K. (2012, July). The Assets Between Your Ears. *Washington Monthly*, 44(7), pp. 33-34.

[30] Colleges, Association of Canadian Community. Post Secondary Transfers. May 2010. 11 October 2012 <http://www.accc.ca/ftp/briefs-memoires/201005_SocialAffairs.pdf>.

[31] Edinsburg School of Business. (2012). Applications and Admissions. Retrieved from ebsglobal.net: http://www.ebsglobal.net/programmes/mba-distance-learning-admissions

[32] Engineer Leader. (2011). Patience. Persistence. Perseverance. Retrieved from www.engineerleader.com: http://www.engineerleader.com/?p=1110

[33] Faisal, Sharif. Financial Post. 12 September 2012. 11 October 2012 <http://business.financialpost.com/2012/09/11/collaboration-essential-to-overcome-skills-shortage/?__lsa=9d4c82f0>.

[34] Forbes. (2012, 05 14). The Student Employment Gap for the Class of 2012. Retrieved from forbes.com: http://www.forbes.com/sites/danschawbel/2012/05/14/the-student-employment-gap-for-the-class-of-2012/

[35] Freakonomics. (2008, 09 29). Do Good Grades Predict Success? Retrieved from freakonomics.com: http://www.freakonomics.com/2008/09/29/do-good-grades-predict-success/

[36] Giziene, V., Simanaviciene, Z., & Palekiene, O. (2012). Evaluation of Investment in Human Capital Economic Effectiveness. *Engineering Economics*, 23(2), pp. 106-116.

[37] Graduate Management Admission Council. (2008, 01). Proof Positive: Study Underscores GMAT® Validity. Retrieved from gmac.com: http://www.gmac.com/why-gmac/gmac-news/gmnews/2008/january/proof-positive-study-underscores-gmat-validity

[38] Halvorson, H. G. (2011, 02 25). Nine Things Successful People Do Differently. Retrieved from blogs.hbr.org: http://blogs.hbr.org/cs/2011/02/nine_things_successful_people.html

[39] HR Voice. (2012, 02 17). Training the Workforce: How Canada Measures Up in Skills and Job Training. Retrieved from www.hrvoice.org: http://www.hrvoice.org/training-the-workforce-how-canada-measures-up-in-skills-and-job-training/

[40] Lehrer, J. (2011, 03 14). Which Traits Predict Success? (The Importance of Grit). Retrieved from wired.com: http://www.wired.com/wiredscience/2011/03/what-is-success-true-grit/

[41] Lopper, J. (2010, 06 06). Success Factors from Psychology Studies on How to be Successful. Retrieved from suite101.com: http://suite101.com/article/success-factors-from-psychology-studies-on-how-to-be-successful-a245313

[42] M Live. (2011, 12 28). Employment outlook improving in 2012; more employers willing to train, more workers quitting for better jobs. Retrieved from mlive.com: http://www.mlive.com/jobs/index.ssf/2011/12/employment_outlook_improving_in_2012_mor.html

[43] Mashable. (2012, 06 17). 4 Business School Trends to Watch. Retrieved from mashable.com: http://mashable.com/2012/06/17/business-school-trends/?utm_source=feedburner&utm_medium=feed&utm_campaign=Feed%3A+Mashable+%28Mashable%29&utm_content=Google+Reader

[44] Millenial Branding. (2012, 05 14). Millennial Branding and Experience Inc. Study Reveals an Employment Gap Between Employers and Students. Retrieved from millennialbranding.com: http://millennialbranding.com/2012/05/millennial-branding-student-employment-gap-study/

[45] Miner, Rick. Miner and Miner. March 2011. 11 October 2012 <http://minerandminer.ca/data/TD_Access_Report.pdf>.

[46] NACE. (2011, 10 28). Job Outlook: The Candidate Skills/Qualities Employers Want. Retrieved from naceweb.org: http://www.naceweb.org/s10262011/candidate_skills_employer_qualities/

[47] Palatnick, F. (2011). Non Traditional Colleges Are Allowing Non Traditional Entrances. Retrieved from http://www.evolllution.com/opinions/non-traditional-colleges-are-allowing-non-traditional-entrances/

[48] Schwartz, S. (2012, 04 30). LSAT Requirement May Be Eliminated. Retrieved from lsatblog.blogspot.ca: http://lsatblog.blogspot.ca/2012/04/lsat-requirement-may-be-eliminated.html

[49] Scott, S. (2007, 08 30). Do grades really matter? Retrieved from macleans.ca: http://www.macleans.ca/education/postsecondary/article.jsp?content=2007091 0_109139_109139

[50] Steinke, J. P. (2009, April). Getting Credit for Life. *Certification Magazine*, 11(4), pp. 22-25.

[51] The Conference Board of Canada. (2010, 01). Education and Skills. Retrieved 06 16, 2012, from http://www.conferenceboard.ca/hcp/Details/education.aspx#canada_right

[52] The Conference Board of Canada. (2012). Employability Skills 2000+. Retrieved from conferenceboard.ca: http://www.conferenceboard.ca/topics/education/learning-tools/employability-skills.aspx

[53] College, B. V. (2011). about TOWES. Retrieved May 1, 2011, from TOWES: http://www.towes.com/en/about-towes/what-is-towes/what-is-towes

[54] College, B. V. (2009). TOWES Data Analysis. Calgary: Bow Valley College.

[55] Myers Briggs Personality Type. (n.d.). Retrieved May 1, 2011, from Myers Briggs: http://www.teamtechnology.co.uk/tt/t-articl/mb-simpl.htm

[56] Scale, E. R. (n.d.). About the ERS. Retrieved May 1, 2011, from Employment Readiness Scale: http://www.employmentreadiness.com/client/default.cfm?wp=ue

[57] WOWI. (2011). Administration. Retrieved May 1, 2011, from WOWI: http://www.wowi.com/

Citizen-to-Soldier-to-Citizen and Cyber Warrior: Building the Cybersecurity Workforce with Military Veterans

Charles E. Wilson, University of Detroit Mercy

Author Note

Correspondence concerning this paper should be addressed to Charles E. Wilson

Center for Cyber Security and Intelligence Studies
Department of Criminal Justice

4001 W. McNichols Street, Detroit, MI 48221

Contact: wilsonce@udmercy.edu

Abstract - The cyber threats facing America have escalated sharply in recent years and has emerged as a clear and present danger to the nation's homeland and national security, economic prosperity, intellectual capital, and critical infrastructure. In the face of such persistent and escalating cyber threats, the United States is determined to immediately develop the capability necessary to counter this threat. A key component of the national cybersecurity strategy includes building a qualified cybersecurity workforce with the competence, knowledge, and technical skills. The cyber workforce must be capable when necessary to not only respond to, effectively counter, and eventually prevent the occurrence of cyber attacks. This paper argues that the U.S. has an untapped resource that will enhance its ability to meet the cybersecurity workforce requirements. That resource is the available military veterans who have served this country with distinction and honor. Most veterans have demonstrated through their service that they possess the necessary potential, characteristics and experience to successfully participate in the cybersecurity workforce. This paper postulates that the cybersecurity workforce can be rapidly filled by focusing efforts on the recruitment, education, and employment of military veterans.

Keywords: Military veterans, cybersecurity, cyber threats, national security, and cybersecurity workforce

INTRODUCTION

This paper reflects the synthesis of empirical data gathered from an extensive review of research literature, open source government documents, and real world case studies culled from media reports and academic research materials. The paper will present the information in four sections: First, by highlighting the scope of the cybersecurity problem. Second, by presenting the American cybersecurity agenda developed to address the problem. Third, by describing the specific and unique characteristics, traits, and experiences gaining through military service that make the veteran an excellent candidate for the cybersecurity workforce. Fourth, by offering recommendations and options to facilitate the recruitment, education, and employment processes for military veterans seeking to enter the cybersecurity workforce. Because, the country is facing an increasing number of sophisticated cyber threats, there is a dire need to address the personnel shortfall of over one million qualified cybersecurity professionals. This paper suggests that the recruitment, education and employment of military veterans are a viable solution to this mounting problem.

This paper offers thought-provoking suggestions for tackling the cybersecurity workforce issue. The paper argues that the cybersecurity workforce can be rapidly filled by focusing efforts on the recruitment, education, and employment of military veterans. Because of their military pedigree and experience veterans can play a pivotal role in the next chapter of American cybersecurity prevention efforts. There is likely one question on the minds of the readers of this paper – what is it that makes veterans so special and unique when compared to any other job candidates? A recent study by Syracuse University's Institute for Veterans and Military Families (2012) presented a robust, specific, and compelling business case for hiring individuals with military background and experience. The report concluded that empirical research from multiple fields and disciplines, such as business, psychology, sociology, and national security support the hiring of military veterans. The report noted that military veterans bring a unique set of knowledge, skills, and abilities that can enhance organizational performance and provide a competitive advantage in the dynamic business environment.

The aforementioned report, "The Business Case for Hiring a Veteran," identified specific characteristics that many veterans possess that help them excel in the workplace. The authors found, that veterans "exhibit high levels of resiliency, advanced team building skills, and strong organizational commitment" (p. 2). Additional, evidence of support for a focused cybersecurity workforce education and employment program for military veterans is included in the following sections of the paper.

SCOPE OF THE THREAT

The stark reality of the cybersecurity threat is manifested on a daily basis with repeated reports of cyber attacks being reported by both the private sector and the federal government. Since 2002, there have been a large number of advanced, well-orchestrated attacks against private sector, military and government information technology systems. The Computer Security Institute's, Computer Crime and Security Survey (Power, 2002) of large corporations and government agencies revealed that:

- 90 percent of respondents had detected computer security breaches;
- 80 percent of respondents had suffered financial losses as a result of computer breaches;
- 85 percent of respondents had detected computer viruses; and
- 78 percent of respondents had detected employees' abuse of Internet access privileges (e.g., downloading pornography or pirated software, or inappropriate use of e-mail systems).
- 75 percent of respondents cited their Internet connection as a frequent point of attack, and
- 33 percent cited their internal systems as a frequent point of attack.

Researchers Virilis, Serrano, and Dandurand (2014) categorized contemporary cyber attacks as advanced persistent threats (APT) with unique characteristics that differentiate them from traditional attacks. It is the combination of complexity, sophistication, and innovation that exacerbates the situation and elevates the contemporary cyber threat attacks to that of a top tier national security threat and critical business issue. Virilis et al., (2014) further suggested that cyber attackers employing APTs frequently use zero-day exploits or modified and obfuscated cyber attack methods to evade the majority of signature-based end points and network intrusion detection solutions. This reinforces the criticality of building a competent cybersecurity workforce capable of minimizing, countering and preventing cyber attacks. America must make every effort to mobilize its available resources to address a continuous growing menace that is becoming more capable with each attack.

In April 2009, a reporter for the Wall Street Journal wrote in a front page story that the networks that control the electricity grid in the U.S. had been penetrated by Russian and Chinese cyber-spies (Gorman, 2009). Additionally, USA TODAY reported that federal records showed that cyberattacks on U.S. government computer networks increased by 40 percent that year (Eisler, 2009). In 2010, numerous Fortune 500 companies reported a wave of new and sophisticated attacks against U.S. industry. Google (Arrington, 2010) announced that it, along with more than 70 high-tech companies, had lost important intellectual property. That same year, Exxon-Mobil, Marathon, and Conoco-Phillips also revealed their systems had been penetrated by sophisticated nation-state actors (Clayton, 2010).

Recent attacks on various U.S. government entities (Inserra & Rosenzweig, 2014), private sector enterprises, and critical infrastructure assets, such as Google, Sony, Target, JP Morgan, and Chase emphasize the urgency of acquiring the capacity to prevent such attacks. Moreover, alarm continued to rise when in 2011 the Office of the National Counterintelligence Executive (ONCIX) reported that "foreign economic collection and industrial espionage against the United States represent significant and growing threats to the nation's prosperity and security." In 2013, the cybersecurity firm Mandiant disclosed that hundreds of terabytes of data from 141 companies in 20 different industries had been stolen remotely by hackers in China. According to the Symantec (2014) Internet Security Treat Report there were more than 41 million attacks detected, eight mega breaches, and 253 total breaches which exposed over 552 million personal identification of end users. (p. 14) Large retailers like Staples Inc., Neiman Marcus Inc., Michaels, Home Depot Inc. and eBay Inc. announced breaches, where millions of customers' credit card information and personal data were stolen by cyber attackers. But it wasn't just retail giants: Firms in health care (Community Health Systems), finance (JPMorgan Chase & Co.) and entertainment (Sony Pictures) were also victims to cyberattacks. In addition to breaches, attacks, other major software vulnerabilities also surfaced: (1) The Open SSL Heartbleed vulnerability shook confidence in Internet security; and (2) Shellshock exposed a majority of Internet-facing services to attack (Steinberg, 2014). Many cybersecurity experts stated that these two Internet attacks are prime examples of the serious cyber threats menacing critical elements of the Internet and the global information infrastructure. Moreover, these two cyber attacks add evidence to the argument that building a capable cybersecurity workforce is an absolutely essential element for the protection of the cyberspace environment. For example, Jose Pagliery (2014) noted that when Heartbleed was discovered, the Internet security function (Open SSL) was maintained by a handful of volunteers, only one of whom worked full-time.

At the individual level over 556 million people per year are victims of cybercrime, 1.5 million per hour, 18 people per second, and with an annual price of $110 billion (McAfee, 2014). This figure represents 46 % of online adults who have been victims of cybercrime in the past twelve months, compared with the findings from 2011 at 45 percent (Symantec). In total, cybercrime costs the world significantly more than the global black market in marijuana, cocaine, and heroin combined. McAfee (2014) estimated that the likely annual cost to the global economy from cybercrime is more than $400 billion. They further estimated that the range of losses would be between $375 billion and as much as $575 billion. According to Kaspersky Lab (2012), cyber criminals launched 1.5 billion web attacks throughout 2012, used 6.5 million unique domains (2.5 million more than in 2011), and seeded malicious code into Internet servers and zones of 202 countries around the world.

A Government Accounting Office (GAO) report (2012) noted that the number and complexity of cyber-attacks has been increasing steadily in recent years. For instance, the report stated that cyber attacks on the Federal Government alone increased 680% from 2006 to 2011 Moreover, according to a recent survey more than 60 percent of IT experts interviewed by the Pew

Internet and American Life Project, a major cyberattacks will happen between now and 2025. . The rise in the number of cybersecurity attacks and the increasing sophistication of the various methods used to perpetrate many of the cyber intrusions means that the traditional, education and human resource models used to educate and employ cybersecurity workforce must be modified. The country cannot afford to wait until the "cyber Pearl Harbor" predicted by the former Secretary of Defense Leon E. Panetta (2012).

According to a report from Verizon "Data Breach Investigations" (Baker, 2014), the most common cybersecurity crimes come from various small online attacks, such as people clicking on malicious web links and choosing easy-to-guess passwords. The Verizon report is one of the top annual reports of Internet-related crime, it includes information from more than 50 organizations around the world and is used to analyze more than 63,000 security incidents and 1,300 confirmed breaches. Verizon analyzed 10 years of data breach data, and specifically stated that most organizations cannot keep up with cybercrime, and the bad guys are winning. The above examples of cyberattacks provide a sobering explanation for why it is so important that the country rapidly formulate a comprehensive and proactive strategy to recruit, prepare, train and educate, and then deploy a competent cybersecurity workforce.

The above noted array of information, statistics, and data illustrate the mounting threat presented by the contemporary malevolent attackers in the cyber space. Clearly, the threats in cyber space are growing in frequency, severity, sophistication, and level of risk. The cyber space threat encompasses a broad spectrum of activities including cyber crime, cyber terrorism, and cyber espionage. A comprehensive and systematic cybersecurity strategy is sorely needed to counter this threat in an effective and efficient manner. An essential component to an effective solution will also require the growth and sustainment of a capable cybersecurity workforce. The pool of available military veterans offers the country a viable and valuable resource that should and can be tapped immediately for the cybersecurity workforce.

THE UNITED STATES NATIONAL CYBERSECURITY AGENDA

Clearly, securing American cyberspace means that the country must develop a technologically-skilled workforce comprised of educated cyber-skilled personnel, and establish an effective pipeline of future employees. Billions of dollars are spent on new technologies to help secure the U.S. in cyberspace. However, it will also take a national strategy, similar to the effort to upgrade science and mathematics education in the 1950's, to meet the challenge of securing cyberspace. The Bush administration addressed the cybersecurity threat by formulating and implementing the Comprehensive National Cybersecurity Initiative (CNCI) in National Security Presidential Directive 54/Homeland Security Presidential Directive 23 (NSPD-54/HSPD-23).

Upon taking office in 2008, President Barack Obama stated that the cybersecurity risk faced by America was a serious economic and national security threat. The President ordered a thorough review of federal efforts to defend the U.S. information and communications infrastructure and the development of a comprehensive approach to securing the nation's digital infrastructure. President Obama determined that the CNCI initiatives should become key elements of a comprehensive U.S. national cybersecurity strategy. These CNCI will play a key role in supporting the achievement of many of the key recommendations of the Cyberspace Policy Review. The Cyberspace Policy Review published in May 2009, concluded that our information technology and communications infrastructure was extremely vulnerable and that numerous attacks have resulted in the loss of hundreds of millions of dollars to cyber criminals. Additionally, the policy review noted that nation-states and other non-state entities have stolen vital intellectual property from the private sector, and sensitive national security and military information.

The CNCI consists of mutually reinforcing initiatives with the major goals of securing the United States in cyberspace: (1) to establish a front line of defense against today's immediate threats by creating or enhancing shared situational awareness of network vulnerabilities, threats, and events... and the ability to act quickly to reduce our current vulnerabilities and prevent intrusions. (2) To defend against the full spectrum of threats by enhancing U.S. counterintelligence capabilities and increasing the security of the supply chain for key information technologies. (3) To strengthen the future cybersecurity environment by expanding cyber education… and develop strategies to deter hostile or malicious activity in cyberspace. Specifically, CNCI Initiative #8 "Expand cyber education" is the core function that must be effectively implemented to ensure the successful staffing and sustainment of a quality cybersecurity workforce.

The National Initiative for Cybersecurity Education (NICE) was established to lead the effort aimed at meeting the goals outlined in CNCI Initiative 8, which addresses the nation's cybersecurity needs related to public awareness, education, professional development, and talent management. In simple terms, the need for cybersecurity specialists is growing exponentially due to increasing criminal, state-sponsored, and terrorist threats. Currently, there are not enough cybersecurity professionals to meet the volume and ever-changing nature of cybersecurity work. Compounding the gap between need and available workforce is the length of time cybersecurity specialists need to adequately develop the necessary skills. The cybersecurity field necessitates that its practitioners grow, evolve, and maintain highly-technical skills that take a significant amount of time to mature. Therefore, it is imperative that both the government and private sector organizations practice effective workforce planning in cybersecurity.

Congress codified the nation's cybersecurity policy by enacting the Cybersecurity Enhancement Act of 2010 (HR 4061), which authorized "hundreds of millions of dollars for cybersecurity research and education." This appropriation included funding for the National Science Foundation "to increase the size and skills of the cybersecurity workforce" and aimed to increase "research and development, standards development and coordination, and public outreach" in cybersecurity. Congress subsequently enacted follow-on legislation in the form of The National Cybersecurity and Critical Infrastructure Protection Act of 2014. Within that Act two specific sections are focused countering the cybersecurity threat. First, Title I: Securing the Nation Against Cyber Attack - (Sec. 102) amends the Homeland Security Act of 2002 (HSA) to require the Secretary of Homeland Security to conduct cybersecurity activities, including the provision of shared situational awareness among federal entities to enable real-time, integrated, and operational actions to protect from, prevent, mitigate, respond to, and recover from cyber incidents. Second, Title III: Homeland Security Cybersecurity Workforce - (Sec. 301) amends the HSA to add provisions entitled the Homeland Security Cybersecurity Boots-on-the-Ground Act, requiring the Secretary of the Department of Homeland Security (DHS) to: (1) develop occupation categories for individuals performing activities in furtherance of DHS's cybersecurity mission, (2) ensure that such categories may be used throughout DHS and are made available to other federal agencies, and (3) conduct an annual assessment of the readiness and capacity of the DHS workforce to meet its cybersecurity mission.

It is evident that the United States government and its policy makers have recognized that existing and emerging cybersecurity threats are menacing the country on a daily basis. Both President Obama and Congress have put forth national policies and implementing actions to build the nation's cybersecurity capabilities and workforce staffing. National efforts to address the cyber-based needs include the establishment of federally funded programs, initiatives, and systematic approaches that serve as a viable launching platform for the strategy to enhance the recruitment, education and retention of the US cybersecurity workforce. However, there are still significant deficiencies that must be addressed if America is going to be successful in cyberspace.

In 2000, the National Science Foundation (NSF) implemented the Scholarship for Service program (SFS) to fund undergraduate and post-graduate students' education in exchange for employment in a Federal, State, Local, or Tribal government's IT workforce after graduation. In December 2011, the National Science and Technology Council partnered with the NSF to expand the coordinated federal strategy and program for cybersecurity education and employment. The joint federal effort was built around two focused tracks: *Scholarship Track and Capacity Track*. The *Scholarship Track* provides funding to colleges and universities for scholarships to students studying in the information assurance and cybersecurity fields. The *Capacity*

Building Track, provides funds to colleges and universities to improve the quality and increase the production of high-quality information assurance and cybersecurity professionals by providing support for education efforts within higher education institutions teaching Science, Technology, Engineering and Mathematics (STEM) disciplines (National Science Foundation, 2014). The federal funds available from these two tracks can be combined with the veteran's benefits provided by the G.I. Bill for education to enhance the overall education process. Moreover, this combined scholarship/stipend package can serve as a motivational incentive for the interested and qualified veterans to enter the cyber education pipeline and continue into the cybersecurity workforce. An additional incentive could include the establishment of a retention/performance bonus based on years of service, excellent performance, continued professional development, and for remaining in the cyber workforce for a specified period of time.

At approximately the same time, the Department of Defense started a similar effort, the Information Assurance Scholarship Program (IASP). Both programs also provide capacity-building grants to academic institutions to bolster cyber security education and workforce development. Nevertheless, the efforts to date have failed to adequately recruit, educate, and employ sufficient numbers of qualified cyber-skilled personnel to meet the nation's needs. Therefore, this paper argues that another approach is warranted that involves focusing human resources and education efforts on integrating military veterans into building the nation's cybersecurity workforce. The innovative use of programs, such as Scholarship Track and Capacity Track can enable the education pipeline to increase the number of students of the United States higher education enterprise to produce cybersecurity professionals. Moreover, these types of focused approaches to cyber education and employment are especially suited for bringing the military veteran into the cyber education process and subsequently into the cybersecurity workforce.

THE MILITARY VETERAN: A CYBERSECURITY WORKFORCE SOLUTION

The U.S military is comprised of the Army, Navy, Air Force, Coast Guard, and Marine Corps, which are all under the command of the U.S. President as Commander in Chief. Over the country's history the military has played a vital role in the geopolitical arena of international affairs related to national security and defense. The U. S. military has evolved with America from a new nation fighting Great Britain for independence (1775–83); through the historical American Civil War (1861–65); through two World Wars, and numerous other smaller conflicts (The Korean War and the War in Viet Nam); the Cold War era (1945 – 91); and the War on Terrorism (2001–present) (HQDA, 2003). U.S. Statutory law, 38 U.S.C. § 101 defines a veteran as an individual who served in the active military, naval, or air service, and who was discharged or released under honorable conditions.. For the purposes of this paper, a veteran is defined as anyone who served on active duty in any job capacity while a member of the Army, Navy, Air Force, Marines or Coast Guard active components, or of the National Guard or Reserves, and was not discharged dishonorably.

Today, America is often described as the world's sole remaining superpower of the 21st century. The remarkable fact is that as great as the country has been and as great as it is, its military force has always consisted of citizens who are willing to serve and defend the nation. It is the citizen-turned-soldier serving as a dedicated member of the nation's military who has demonstrated the character, honor, sense of duty, and sacrifice necessary to make America great. The premise of this paper's thesis is that it is the cultivation of the military culture that serve as the incubator of the military veteran's unique experience, knowledge, skills, and intellectual capacities. Moreover, it is the development and reinforcement of the tenets of the military culture that contributes to the growth of a system of beliefs that manifest themselves as invaluable attributes like leadership, accountability, resiliency, problem solving, and adaptability in these veterans.

Over America's history there are numerous examples of military veterans who have risen to the occasion and helped the country through some very trying times. Former military personnel have long had successful careers in both the public and private sectors, following their return to civilian life. Many of these men and women have left an indelible mark on American history, rising to the upper echelons of U.S. government - Presidents George Washington, Ulysses S. Grant, Dwight D. Eisenhower, Theodore Roosevelt, Harry S. Truman, John F. Kennedy, Jimmy Carter, and Ronald Reagan were all military veterans. For these reasons and others, Americans have more confidence in the military than any other institution or group in the country. The American confidence is well placed, and it is in our Nation's interest to continue to invest in our military veterans. They have much to offer our communities long after they hang up the uniform (Mendes & Wilke, 2013).

While the vast majority of veterans are not going to become president, in general they strengthened our country by their service and as a result, are civic assets with great potential to continue serving and leading in our communities, businesses, and governments. Examples of veterans continuing to serve abound, all you have to do is look for them. Consider the following examples in the private sector and the corporate world, where veterans are represented by the likes of Alex Gorsky, the chief executive and chairman of Johnson & Johnson, and Bob McDonald, who guided Procter & Gamble to extraordinary growth while serving as its chairman, president, and chief executive, from 2009 to 2013. Another noted military veteran who has provided service while occupying a key civilian positions is retired General Colin Powell, former Chairman of the Joint Chiefs of Staff and Secretary of State. Moreover, business representatives report that hiring veterans is good business, according to detailed and lengthy interviews with 87 individuals representing 69 companies. The companies cited numerous reasons for hiring military veterans, with an emphasis on veterans' leadership and teamwork skills, character, discipline, and expertise (Harrell & Berglass, 2012).

Further examples of the value added contribution of military veterans include the following individuals. David Oclander, an army veteran, who moved to Chicago to help disadvantaged kids in the tough neighborhoods in the city. He is now a Principal Fellow at the Noble Network of Charter Schools (Warner, 2014). David's service after the military has helped the Noble Network schools achieve an overall college matriculation rate of 90% and eight of their ten campuses ranked among the top ten schools based on ACT performance in 2014. Tammy Duckworth was one of the first Army women to fly combat missions during Operation Iraqi Freedom until her helicopter was hit by an RPG (Carter and Almasy, 2013). She lost her legs and partial use of her right arm in the explosion. Despite these injuries, she continued to serve our Nation, first as an Assistant Secretary of Veterans Affairs and now as a Congresswoman for Illinois's 8th Congressional District (Office of the Joint Chiefs of Staff, 2014). Or consider Jacob Wood, who honorably served four years in the Marine Corps, deploying to Iraq in 2007 and Afghanistan in 2008. He graduated Scout-Sniper School at the top of his class and in 2007 he was awarded the Navy and Marine Corps Commendation Medal with "V" for actions in Iraq. Following his service in the Marines, Jake co-founded Team Rubicon, a non-profit disaster relief organization that puts veteran volunteers to work in responding to disasters around the world (Martinez, 2015). Jacob Wood is another example of the service pedigree that resides within most military veterans. Veterans often continue their faithful service by channeling their unwavering commitment and dedication to fulfill critical needs in their communities.

These few examples represent the immense potential that most veterans have to continue serving after they've hung up their uniform. They are counted among the many veterans who have demonstrated the competencies, traits, and leadership skills they acquired while serving in the military and later in essential civilian roles. Empirical support for reintegration of veterans into the cybersecurity workforce includes academic research from the fields of business, psychology, and sociology. In general, the literature strongly links characteristics that are generally representative of military veterans to enhanced performance and organizational advantage in the context of a competitive and dynamic business environment (Cooker, 2014). In other words, the academic research supports a robust, specific, and compelling argument for hiring individuals with military background and experience (Berglass & Harrell,

2012). According to Steve Cooker, more than two-thirds of employers report having special talent needs that a veteran candidate would be more qualified to fill than a non-veteran candidate. So employers recognize the unique skills that veterans possess.

THE GI BILL: THE EDUCATION ENABLER

Because America felt a moral obligation to help prepare our veterans to live a fulfilling life after they have served honorably, the country established the first GI Bill of Rights in 1944, which was signed into law by President Franklin D. Roosevelt. Almost eight million veterans took advantage of the education and training benefits it offered. Since the establishment of the first GI Bill millions of veterans from later conflicts benefited from similar measures. Seventy-one years after the first GI Bill was signed, Congress passed the Post-9/11 Veterans Educational Assistance Act. The Post-9/11 GI Bill expands the educational benefits of the original GI Bill, providing veterans with full funds to attend a public undergraduate program for four years, with additional stipends for housing and books. A review of available statistics reveals that each version of the G.I. Bill had an important and positive influence on improving the lives of returning veterans, by providing access to higher education. A significant number of each generation of military veterans have avail themselves to G.I. Bill education benefits. A greater percentage of Vietnam veterans used G.I. Bill education benefits (72 percent) than World War II veterans (51 percent) or Korean War veterans (43 percent). More recently, the Post-9/11 G.I. Bill has paid for nearly 1 million veterans of the Iraq and Afghanistan wars to go to school at a cost of about $30 billion since 2009 (Wagner, Cave, & Winston, 2013).

On August 3, 2009, President Barack Obama attended a ceremony marking the creation of the GI Bill benefits program over sixty-five years earlier. During the ceremony he acknowledged the contributions of military veterans over the history of the country in both peace and war. The president noted that education is the currency that can purchase success in the 21st century, and that the opportunity to participate in the education process was earned by our military veterans. In November 2009, President Obama further acknowledged both the service of military veterans by issuing an executive order promoting the recruitment and employment of veterans within the Federal Government. The executive order established an interagency Council on Veterans Employment, which is co-chaired by the Secretaries of Labor and Veterans Affairs. In support of this initiative, the Federal Government have established various websites to assist veterans with employment and training opportunities.

Applicants for military service must meet academic, moral, and physical requirements that disqualify most of their peers. In fact, only 25 percent of Americans ages 17 to 24 are physically, mentally, and morally qualified for military service (Gilroy, 2013). According to the U. S. Census Bureau (2012) all Army and Marine Corps and 99% of Air Force and Navy enlisted personnel accessions were high school graduates in FY 2012. Consequently, a higher percentage of veterans ages 25 and over have a high school diploma than their non-veteran counterparts. According to Thomas Meyer from Philanthropy Roundtable noted, the current generation of service members "exceed national norms, on average, in education and intelligence, health and character qualities." In sum, the current generation of veterans exceeds, on average, national norms in education and intelligence; moreover, more veterans seek some post-secondary education than do their non-veteran peers. These facts are strong evidence that the nation's military veterans possess the necessary knowledge, skills, abilities, and potential to successfully meet the requirements for completion of education and employment in the cybersecurity workforce.

There is a recognized persistent national shortage of skilled cyberspace personnel that negatively impacts the social, economic and political dimensions across the nation and potentially putting national security at risk (Evans & Reeder, 2010). In response to this challenge, America must expand education and employment opportunities to cultivate talent from within the available personnel most capable of successfully completing the rigors and challenges of an aggressive education process. The military veteran is uniquely qualified to cope with the stressors, mental and physical conditions, and academic endurance necessary to complete the cyber security educational program.

The military profession is unlike any other profession. The demands of military life creates and reinforces a unique set of personal qualities and attributes in its service members built on the inculcation of professionalism, ethics, ethos, and belief in a value system. In the military every service members' performance is evaluated and all members are developed, counseled and mentored throughout their career. The military emphasizes discipline and order, priority of the group over the individual, and use of specific rituals and symbols to convey important meanings and transitions. For example, the Army emphasizes seven (7) core values to establish and instill a shared set of beliefs, way of thinking and behavior expectations in every soldier:

- **Loyalty** – Bear true faith and allegiance to the U.S. Constitution, the Army, your unit, and fellow Soldiers.

- **Duty** – Fulfill your obligations. Accept responsibility for your own actions and those entrusted to your care.

- **Respect** – Treat others as they should be treated.

- **Selfless Service** – Put the welfare of the nation, the Army, and your subordinates before your own.

- **Honor** – Live the Army Values.

- **Integrity** – Do what's right, both legally and morally.

- **Personal Courage** – Face fear, danger, or adversity, both physical and moral.

Each of the military branches has established and consistently reinforced a pattern of behaviors based on a set of beliefs that epitomizes its cultural system. The military culture is instilled and reinforced in each service member from the very first day that each of them takes their oath of oath of enlistment and oath of office (for commissioned officers). Moreover, within each service there is a constant emphasis on core values which serve as a normative guide for personal and professional behavior patterns. Service members learn these values in detail during initial training, and from then on they are expected to live them every day in everything they do - whether they're on duty or off. These values are the building blocks for the military culture and the most fundamental element of the institutional identity of the military services. The Army's

Training and Doctrine Command Culture Center (2007) defines culture as a "dynamic social system," containing the values, beliefs, behaviors, and norms of a "specific group, organization, society or other collectivity" learned, shared, internalized… by all members of that society. Another way of stating this is by using the term "cultural competence" which implies that an individual is able to perform effectively in a number of diverse environments and refers to an ability to interact effectively with people of different cultures and socio-economic backgrounds (Chamberlain, 2005). This paper argues that the dynamics of exposure, acceptance, faithfulness, and routine performance of duties pursuant to the principles and tenets of the military culture makes the military veteran an excellent candidate for cybersecurity education for the express purpose of employment in the cyber security workforce.

RECOMMENDATIONS FOR THE WAY AHEAD

- Create a national cybersecurity clearinghouse for veterans, key stakeholders, private sector entities and higher education communities – for the sharing of knowledge, resources, education and employment opportunities to help increase cybersecurity capabilities, and optimizing collaboration to eliminate unnecessary duplication.

- Establish an aggressive education and employment outreach and support program aimed specifically at recruiting and training military veterans for these cybersecurity workforce.

- Maximize use of social media and networking to enhance the reintegration process for military veterans.

- To aid in translating military skills and facilitate the transition process, DOD, DHS and the Department of Veterans Affairs (VA) should seek public-private partnerships with American companies and qualified nonprofit organizations that specialize in employment and supporting veterans.

- Create both national and regional education consortiums to serve as national facilitators and advocators for cybersecurity education.

- DOD and Department of Labor (OL should provide guidance for companies to help them interpret which veteran candidates were successful, or even highly successful, in performing their duties while in uniform.

CONCLUSION

As explained above, most veterans possess valuable traits, characteristics and attributes that empower them with great potential to serve and lead our nation's communities after their service. Moreover, they are especially capable and very suited for the cyber security workforce. It is important to remember that every service member came from our communities and that they all will return to our communities. America has an obligation to offer our veterans every opportunity to continue their service and become better citizens upon completion of their military service. Otherwise, we might miss an opportunity to incorporate veterans into our cyber security workforce as the essential assets that they are. Veterans via their military service, acquire and/or increase personal qualities, and their sense of duty, therefore, they possess exceptional potential to help fill the gaps and vacancies currently existing in the US cyber-security workforce. America should take advantage of the opportunity to capitalize on a proven human capital asset by focusing a special effort on placing its military veterans into the cybersecurity workforce. America can enhance its cybersecurity capabilities by implementing a proactive and aggressive effort to integration military veterans into the cybersecurity workforce in order to utilize their specialized skills, experiences and training.

REFERENCES

[1] Arrington, M. (2010). Google defense against large scale Chinese cyber attack: May cease Chinese operations. Tech Crunch. Retrieved from http://techcrunch.com/2010/01/12/google-china-attacks/.

[2] Baker, W. (2014). Verizon's data breach investigations report series. Retrieved from http://www.verizonenterprise.com/DBIR/2014/.

[3] Carter, C. J. and Almasy, S. (2013) CNN News Report: Former troops say time has come for women in combat units. Retrieved from http://www.cnn.com/2013/01/23/us/women-combat-troop-reaction/.

[4] Chamberlain, S. P. (2005). Recognizing and responding to cultural differences in the education of culturally and linguistically diverse learners. Intervention in School & Clinic, 40 (4), pp. 195-211.

[5] Clayton, M. (2010). US oil industry hit by cyberattacks: Was China involved? The Christian Science Monitor, 25 January 2010. Retrieved from

http://www.csmonitor.com/USA/2010/0125/US-oil-industry-hit-by-cyberattacks-Was-China.../

[6]   Congress (2014). H.R.3696 - 113th Congress (2013-2014): National cybersecurity and critical infrastructure protection act of 2014 – Title I: securing the nation against cyber Attacks. Retrieved from https://www.congress.gov/bill/113th-congress/house-bill/3696

[7]   Conley, D. T. New conceptions of college and career ready: a profile approach to admission. *Journal of College Admission*, No. 223, April 2014, pp. 12–23.

[8]   Cooker, S. (2014). Fighting veteran unemployment by closing the skills translation gap. Monster.com. Retrieved from http://www.military.com / veteran-jobs / career-advice / 2014 / 11 / 18 / fighting-veteran-unemployed....

[9]   Duckworth, A L., Christopher P., Michael D. M., and Dennis D. R., "Grit: perseverance and passion for long-term Goals," *Journal of Personality and Social Psychology*, Vol. 92, No. 6, 2007, pp. 1087–1101.

[10] Duckworth, A. L., and Patrick D. Q., Development and validation of the short grit scale (Grit-S). *Journal of Personality Assessment*, Vol. 91, No. 2, 2009, pp. 166–174.

[11] Dweck, Carol S., Gregory M. W., and Geoffrey C. L. Academic tenacity: Mindsets and skills that promote long-term learning. Retrieved from http://collegeready.gatesfoundation.org/article/ academic-tenacity-mindsets-and-skills-promote-long-term-learning.

[12] Evans, K. and Reeder, F. (2010). A human capital crisis in cybersecurity – technical proficiency matters. Washington, D.C: April 2010.

[13] Eisler, P. (2009). "Reported raids on federal computer data soar. USA TODAY, 17 February, 2009. Retrieved from http://30.usatoday.com/news/washington/2009-02-16-cyber-attacks_N.html.

[14] Franken, Robert E. *Human Motivation*, 3rd ed., Pacific Grove, Ill.: Brooks/Cole, 1993.

[15] Gilroy, Curtis, Dr. (2009) Statement to the House, Committee on Armed Services, Recruiting, Retention and End Strength Overview, Hearing, March 3, 2009. Retrieved from http://www.gpo.gov/fdsys/pkg/CHRG-111hhrg50088/pdf/CHRG-111hhrg50088.pdf.

[16] Government Accounting Office. Executivegov.com. (2012). Retrieved from http://www.executivegov.com/2012/04/gao-federal-cyberspace-incidents-up-680-over-5-years/.

[17] Gorman, S. (2009). "Electricity grid in U.S. penetrated by spies," Wall Street Journal, 8 April 2009. Retrieved from http://online.wsj.com/article/SB123914805204099085.html.

[18] Griffin, P. E., and Esther C. "Project method overview," Patrick Griffin and Esther Care, eds., Assessment and Teaching of 21st Century Skills, Vol. 2: Methods and Approaches, Dordrecht, the Netherlands: Springer, 2015.

[19] Hamilton, L. S., Heather L. S., Brian S. S., & Steele, J. L. Improving accountability through expanded measures of performance," *Journal of Educational Administration*, Vol. 51, No. 4, 2013, pp. 453–475.

[20] Harrell, M. & Berglass, N. (2012) Employing America's veterans. Military, Veterans and Society Program for a New American Security (CNAS). Retrieved from http://www.cnas.org/files/documents/publications/ (retrieved October 27, 2014).

[21] Headquarters, Department of the Army. (2003) Field Manual, No. 1–20 *Military History Operations*, Washington, DC, 3 February 2003. Retrieved from http://www.train.army.mil

[22] Heckman, J, J. Schools, skills, and synapses," *Economic Inquiry*, Vol. 46, No. 3, July 2008, pp. 289–324.

[23] Inserra, D. and Rosenzweig, P. (2014). Continuing federal cyber breaches warn against

[24] Cybersecurity regulation. Heritage Foundation Issue Brief No. 4288, http://www.heritage.org/research/reports/2014/10/continuing-federal-cyber-breaches-warn-against-cybersecurity-regulation.

[25] Kane, M. T. (2006) *Validation in Educational Measurement*. Robert L. Brennan, ed. 4th ed., Westport, Conn.: Praeger Publishers. pp. 17–64.

[26] Kaspersky Lab. (2012) Security Bulletin: By the Numbers. Retrieved from http://www.kaspersky.com / about / news / virus / 2012 / 2012_by_the_numbers_Kasp....

[27] Martinez, S. (2015). Team Rubicon's co-founder tells West Michigan about the importance of veteran volunteers. The Grand Rapids Press. Retrieved from MLive.com Online. http://www.mlive.com / business / west-Michigan / index.ssf / 2015 / 01 / co-founder_of_team_rubicon...

[28] McAfee (2014). "Net losses: estimating the global cost of cybercrime". Retrieved from http://www.mcafee.com/us/resources/reports/rp-economic-impact-cybercrime2.pdf

[29] Mendes, E. & Wilke, J. (2013). Americans' confidence in congress falls to lowest level on record. Gallup. Retrieved from http://www.gallup.com/poll/163052/americans-confidence-congress-falls-lowest-record.aspx (retrieved Nov. 4, 2014).

[30] Meyer, T. (2013). Serving Those Who Served: A wise giver's guide to assisting veterans and military families. Washington: The Philanthropy Roundtable, 2013, 153.

[31] Moule, Jean (2012). Cultural competence: A primer for educators. Wadsworth/Cengage, Belmont, California.

[32] National Science Foundation. (2013). NSF joins forces with Intel and GE to move the needle in producing U.S. engineers and computer scientists," press release 13-081, May 8, 2013. Retrieved from http://www.nsf.gov/news/news_summ.jsp?cntn_id=127902.

[33] National Science Foundation. (2014). CyberCorps(R) scholarship for service (SFS): Defending

[34] America's cyberspace. Retrieved from http://www.nsf.gov/pubs/2014/nsf14510/nsf14510.htm.

[35] Office of the National Counterintelligence Executive, (2011). Foreign spies stealing U.S. economic secrets in cyberspace: Report to Congress on Foreign Economic Collection and Industrial Espionage, 2009–2011. (ONCIX 2011 Report). Retrieved from http://www.ncix.gov / publications / reports / fecie_all / Foreign_Economic_Collect...

[36] Pagliery, Jose (2014). Your internet security relies on a few volunteers". CNN Money. Cable

[37] News Network.com. Retrieved from http://money.cnn.com/2014/04/18/technology/security/heartbleed-volunteers/

[38] Panetta, L. (2012) Remarks to the business executives for national security. New York City, October 11, 2012. retrieved from www.defense.gov

[39] Pellegrino, J. W., & Margaret L. H. (2012). Education for life and work: Developing transferable knowledge and skills in the 21st Century, Washington, D.C.: National Academies Press.

[40] Power, R. (2002). CSI/FBI computer crime and security survey. *Computer Security Issues and Trends*, vol. 8, no. 1 (Spring 2002).

[41] Saavedra, A. R. & Opfer, D. V. (2012). Learning 21st-century skills requires 21st-Century teaching," Phi Delta Kappan, Vol. 94, No. 2, October 2012, pp. 8–13.

[42] Steinberg, J. (2014). Massive Internet security vulnerability: Here's what you need to do.

[43] Forbes. Retrieved from http://www.forbes.com / sites / joseph steinberg / 2014 / 04 / 10 / massive-internet-security.

[44] Symantec Internet Security Threat Report. (2011). Retrieved from https://www4.symantec.com/mktginfo/downloads/21182883_GA_REPORT_ISTR_Main-Report_04-11_HI-RES.pdf.

[45] Symantec Internet Security Threat Report (2014) Volume 19. Retrieved from http://www.itu.int / en / ITU-D / Cybersecurity / Documents / Symantec_annual_internet....

[46] U.S. Army Training and Doctrine Command Culture Center. (2007). Culture education and training strategy for the U.S. Army. Fort Huachuca, AZ: U.S. Army Intelligence Center.

[47] U.S. Census Bureau (2012). Veteran status, 2012 American community survey estimates. Retrieved from http://factfinder2.census.gov/faces/tableservices/jsf/pages/html.

[48] Virilis, N., Serrano, O., & Dandurand, L. (2014). Big data analytics for sophisticated attack detection. Retrieved from http://www.cis.aueb.gr / Publications / ISACA%20-%20Big%20data%2.

[49] Wagner, M., Cave, A., and Winston, H. (2013). National security: GI bill covered tuition for nearly

[50] a million post-9/11 veterans without tracking their progress. The Center for Public Integrity. Retrieved from http://www.publicintegrity.org / 2013 / 09 / 03 / 13297 / gi-bill-covered-tuition.

[51] Warner, Margaret. (2014). A veteran's tough love message to at-risk kids and fellow vets. PBR News Hour. Retrieved from http://www.youtube.com/watch?v=0hL9F08wRWM .

[52] White House (2009). The Comprehensive national cybersecurity initiative. Retrieved from http://www.whitehouse.gov / issues / foreign-policy / cybersecurity / national-initiative.

[53] White House (2013). Can we instill productive mindsets at scale? A review of the evidence and an initial R&D agenda, white paper prepared for White House

meeting on excellence in education: The importance of academic mindsets. Washington D.C.

[54] Yuan, K. & Vi-Nhuan L. (2014). Measuring deeper learning through cognitively demanding test items: results from the analysis of six national and international exams. RAND Corporation, Santa Monica, Calif. Retrieved from http://www.rand.org/pubs/research_reports/RR483.html.

Conceptual Foundation for UW Center of Academic Excellence in Information Assurance Education[1]

B. Endicott-Popovsky, V. Popovsky, P. Osterli, P. Rosario, S. Nelson

The Center for Information Assurance (IA) and Cybersecurity (CIAC) at the University of Washington, an NSA/DHS Center of Academic Excellence in Information Assurance Education, brings together industry, academia and the Pacific Northwest community to develop cooperative cybersecurity education programs that reflect the region's unique nature: tech-aware, industrially-based, cloud-driven. The programs produce IA professionals at all organizational levels, and across all 31 NICE pathways, who are immediately effective in the work place. A focus of CIAC programs is assisting the 8,000 military a year transitioning through Joint Base Lewis McCord (JBLM), Camp Murray and state-wide Army Reserve Centers, as well as approximately 15,000 veterans that retire annually in Washington State. A large number will enter law enforcement, emergency management and the private sector and can benefit from cybersecurity education. Their 360 awareness and military training make them ideal homeland defenders; however, they need orientation to industry and a soft skill set that prepares them for the different culture and authorities of the private sector. This paper describes the conceptual models that are the foundation of the CIAC that could be replicated.

---

[1] Barbara Endicott-Popovsky, Executive Director for the Center of Information Assurance and Cybersecurity and Professor, Institute of Technology, Academic Director Master of Infrastructure Planning and Management Dept. of Urban Planning, University of Washington;

V.M. Popovsky, Affiliate Professor, School of Education, Department of HERD, University of Idaho;

LTC Philip Osterli, Private-Public Partnership Initiative, Army Reserve Cyber Operations Group.

MAJ Pedro Rosario, Cyber P3i Texas, Army Reserve Cyber Operations Group.

LTC Scott Nelson, Deputy Commanding Officer Army Reserve Cyber Operations Group.

INTRODUCTION

Since the late 1990's, NSA and DHS have encouraged universities to create Centers of Academic Excellence in Information Assurance Education and Research (CAE's and CAE-R's) in order to:

- **Meet national demand** for IA professionals

- **Prepare IA professionals** for national information infrastructure protection

- Provide sources for **IA recruitment**

- Provide sources for **IA research**. [1]

In 2002–2003, the University of Washington sought designation as a Center of Academic Excellence in Information Assurance Education in the under-represented (in terms of CAE's) Pacific Northwest (Figure 1). Through a multidisciplinary collaboration of the Information School, the College of Engineering and the Institute of Technology (UWIT) at Tacoma, CAE status was awarded to UW's Center for Information Assurance and Cybersecurity (CIAC) in 2004.

2002 NSA Centers of Excellence

Figure 1 CIAC in Underrepresented Northwest (Stars represent CAE's in 2002)

The motivation came from Northwest business and government stakeholders who had expressed interest in Information Assurance programs, e.g.: Microsoft had launched its Trustworthy initiative [2]; Boeing Defense and Space was seeking students from programs with IA concentrations; local companies, such as IO Active, were explicitly asking for students with IA and secure coding backgrounds.

In addition, undergraduate and graduate students were demanding IA courses knowing that they needed that knowledge to be competitive in the work place. In response, we created our initial educational offering, the Information Assurance and Risk Management (ISRM) certificate, a three course series of graduate classes that earn a certificate from the CIAC, as well as an academic credential from the university.

IA Professional and Continuing Education Certificates

- Information Systems Security
- Information Security and Risk Management (ISRM)
- Network Engineering
- Digital Forensics
- e-Discovery

Degrees/Tracks/Electives

- Master of Science Info Management IA track
- Informatics network courses
- Tri-campus IA undergrad option
- Master of Science Computer Science - (IA focus)
- Master Cyber Leadership
- Master of Science Cybersecurity
- Master Infrastructure Planning and Management
- PhD Computer Science- IA track (U of Hawaii)

ISRM MOOC (Massive Open Online Course) Coursera

Research Program

- Pacific Northwest National Laboratory MOU- Contracts, Internships

- Interpares Trust University of British Columbia (Canada)

- NSF Scholarship for Service Program/grants

- Fraunhofer Darmstadt (Germany) Collaboration

Outreach

- Unintended Consequences of Information Age Lecture Series (UW TV)

- UW Conferences and Workshops: Honeypots Workshop, Intl Conference on Cloud Security and Management

- Honeynet Alliance Chapter

Pacific Rim Collegiate Cyber Defense Competition (PRCCDC)

Figure 2 UW Cybersecurity Offerings

We have since implemented a series of certificates and degree and research programs over the past decade to meet student and employer demand (Figure 2). In addition, faculty in a variety of disciplines have demonstrated interest in IA research and education, incorporating IA topics in courses and pursuing IA research agendas.

With broad, multi-discipline interest, the Provost Office continues to house the Center which promotes collaboration across schools and campuses. The challenge we faced as the Center grew its offerings was to develop conceptual models that would promote interdisciplinary collaboration and focus on career outcomes for students. Like industry, universities are siloed by discipline.

61

Working interdisciplinarily, across UW campuses, and across sectors: industry, government, and academia requires governance clarity and collaborative relationships that need continuous nurturing. The balance of this paper describes the conceptual foundation underpinning the Center that includes conceptual and operational models that guide activities. We also discuss operational outcomes as an indication of the value of this approach.

CONCEPTUAL FOUNDATION

By bringing together industry, government, and academia, CIAC:

- Promote regional collaboration,
- Produce interdisciplinary research directions and educational programs, and
- Develop IA professionals at all levels who are well- prepared for the work place.

The CIAC's stated mission is to "identify, address, and promote IA solutions as a catalyst for IA research and education, entrepreneurship, invention, public awareness."

In order to produce and promote integrated interdisciplinary programs, the Center employs a system-activity approach developed by Russian and American pedagogues [3, 4, 5, 6, 7, 8, 9, 10]. Some applications and modifications of this approach have been discussed, extensively, in Endicott-Popovsky's previous publications [11, 12, 13, 14, 15, 16, 17, 18, 19, 20].

The CIAC

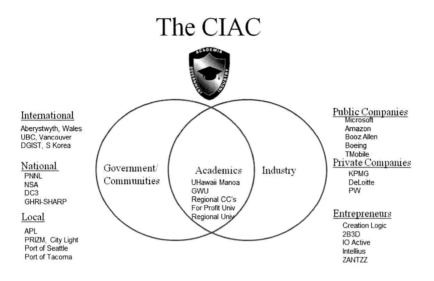

International
Aberystwyth, Wales
UBC, Vancouver
DGIST, S Korea

National
PNNL
NSA
DC3
GHRI-SHARP

Local
APL
PRIZM, City Light
Port of Seattle
Port of Tacoma

Government/
Communities

Academics
UHawaii Manoa
GWU
Regional CC's
For Profit Univ
Regional Univ

Industry

Public Companies
Microsoft
Amazon
Booz Allen
Boeing
TMobile

Private Companies
KPMG
DeLoitte
PW

Entrepreneurs
Creation Logic
2B3D
IO Active
Intellius
ZANTZZ

Figure 3 Integrating Academics, the Community and Industry

The system-activity approach is characterized as follows:

1) Learning occurs through productive activities developed in partnership with the community, academic researchers, and industry. The approach involves _all_ participants - community and industry leaders, university instructors and students, and IA experts - in the learning process. Everyone learns from one another, often creating new knowledge.

2) Emphasis is on student professional development and motivating them to learn more from every possible resource: educational partners throughout the Northwest, certifications, the CIAC's IA network, professional memberships.

3) Knowledge is treated, not as the end goal of the educational process (i.e., learning for a grade), but as a tool to solve practical, complex problems, creatively and independently, unleashing the learner's potential.

4) The end result becomes the personal and professional development of all participants who exhibit creativity, professionalism, and high motivation to learn continuously and independently which helps researchers,

experts, educators, business leaders and students alike stay current in the rapidly evolving field of IA. We encourage reflection on practical experiences, in order to induce generalizations from these experiences and to extend their knowledge.

5) Criteria for measuring the efficiency of this educational approach include contributions to science and industry made by CIAC participants.

This system activity approach is adaptive. The five fundamentals above were implemented as guiding principles for our work, allowing all participants to move rapidly to adjust to evolving learning objectives arising from our fast-paced field.

THE CIAC AS A PEDAGOGICAL SYSTEM

To operationalize the five fundamentals above, the Center is designed, conceptually, as a pedagogical system that produces the following outcomes:

1) Qualified IA professionals who understand current trends, technologies and regulatory policies,,

2) Development of new knowledge and technology,

3) Development of new educational programs, curricula, classroom artifacts (labs, assignments, lectures, etc.)

A major method for achieving these outcomes is integrating recognized IA practitioners into the classroom as guest lecturers and course instructors. This maintains currency of our programs, inspiring students to maintain their knowledge currency. It also makes students triage between the real world and what they learn in books and lectures, which often lags behind what is happening on the 'firing line' in organizations coping with rapidly evolving threats.

The CIAC is conceived as a pedagogical system as depicted in Figure 4 [20]. The Kuzmina-Bespalko–Popovsky (KBP) Pedagogical model is composed of five elements - **students**, **teachers**, **goals**, **content** and **didactic processes** - the first two are intelligent elements, the teacher and the student; the remaining

three are infrastructure elements – the **goals**, **content**, and **didactic processes**
of the curriculum. All elements of the model are dynamic, subject to varying
rates of change and adaptation. All of the elements of the model function as an
interconnected whole and operate within a larger dynamic professional and
social context that includes economic and political environments, as well as a
constantly evolving set of threats, vulnerabilities and operational systems which
are affected by influences such as global competition; technological innovation;
legal policies; and the creativity of business leaders, entrepreneurs and IA
specialists. The context informs the different elements of the model.

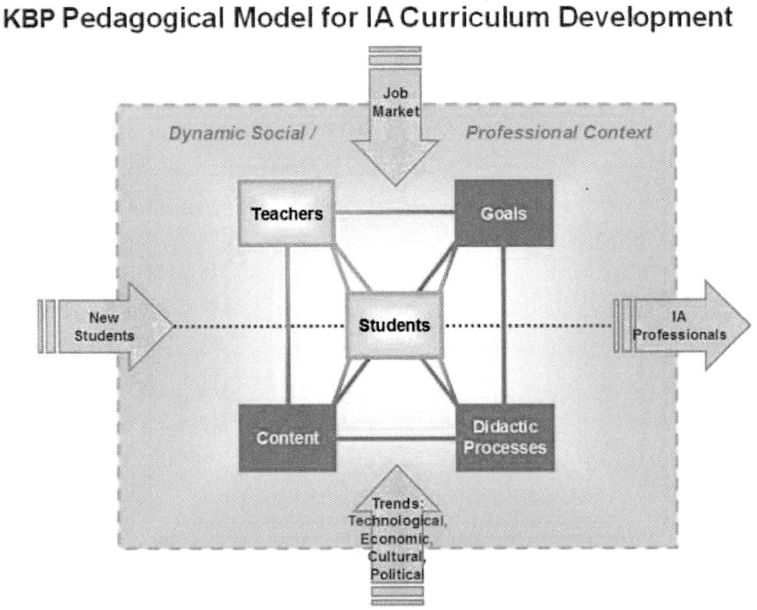

KBP Pedagogical Model for IA Curriculum Development

Figure 4 The KBP Pedagogical Model: CIAC as a pedagogical system [20]

In any given context, a specific instructor with their own specific slice of
IA knowledge and expertise is responsible for developing a specific set of
infrastructure components designed to address the needs of a specific type of
student.

65

Students are central to the model – entering the system as potential IA employees; exiting as IA professionals. By describing each component of the model in relation to learning objectives drawn from the environment and an integration of trends and the condition of the job market, an educational program is developed iteratively. According to Bespalko and Kuzmina, the more precisely the five components are characterized – along with the connections among them – the more repeatable and predictable the learning results [3, 4].

The five elements interact and are changing constantly. Over time, as each of the elements is changed, it affects the other four, requiring each of them to be re-defined, and so on, until all five elements are specified in relation to one another. By continuously updating descriptions of these elements, curriculum is kept current ensuring that students remain competitive. Curriculum is on an annual review cycle, using the model to help think through curricular changes. This process has been described in depth in previous publications [13, 15, 16, 17, 18, 20].

Further the Center relies on the NICE (National Initiative for Cybersecurity Education) to align programs and courses with the 31 pathways defined therein that describe career path required skills and knowledge units. Students are familiarized with NICE to encourage them to drive their own self-study to equip them for the careers they choose [21].

INTERDISCIPLINARY ACADEMIC COOPERATION

Figure 5, is an organizational model for academic interdisciplinary cooperation. Current CIAC members include ten disciplines, administrative functions and partners: the Information School; Tacoma Institute of Technology; University of Washington Bothell; Computer Science and Engineering Department; Electrical Engineering Department, the Daniel J. Evans School of Public Affairs; the Center for Arts, Technology and the Law; the Provost's Office; the Chief Information Security Officer; Professional and Continuing Education; and the Pacific Northwest National Laboratory.

The Center provides an umbrella for current IA research activities of its members, while research is conducted undisturbed within member departments. Collaboration through the Center allows for sharing of information and research results and the development of multi-disciplined research programs. Research is classified within four areas of Information Assurance - Policy, Procedures, Technology and Education/Awareness. The Center provides an umbrella for the current IA research activities of its members, while research is conducted undisturbed within the member departments. Collaboration through the Center allows for sharing of information and research results and the development of multi-disciplined research programs. Research is classified within four areas of Information Assurance - Policy, Procedures, Technology and Education/Awareness.

The Center also serves as a clearinghouse for dissemination of IA research to industry and the local community and for integrating research into the classroom through lectures, workshops, seminars and lab exercises. Ad hoc, solution-oriented committees act as "Rapid-Research-Response teams" to solve emerging problems introduced through member initiatives or by government and industry sponsors (Figure 5).

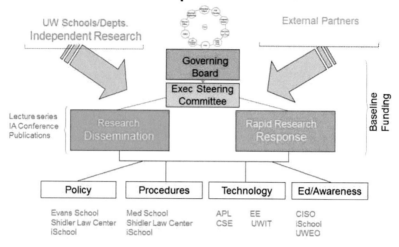

Figure 5 Organizational Model for Research Collaboration through the CIAC

The Center is led by a Governing Board consisting of the leadership from participating faculty and representatives from the Provost's office, the CISO, Pacific Northwest National Labs and other industry and government partners (Figure 6). Board membership grows as the Center expands. The Board provides strategic guidance to the Center and convenes annually with more frequent meetings of an Executive Steering Committee empowered to develop plans and projects for the Center.

An Advisory Board consisting of external leader–collaborators from industry and government engages the community in assisting with resource acquisition and access to funding and internships/jobs for students. The Board draws from a rich set of collaborative relationships forged for various purposes and formalized in memoranda of understanding.

Figure 6 Network of CIAC Collaborators

Since the Center is also a designated CAE-R (Center of Academic Excellence in IA Research), students at all levels of study are involved with Center research offering students unique opportunities to learn from cutting-edge IA leaders. Students learn research methodologies that immerse them in the scientific method, contributing to their development as 'out-of-the-box' IA problem solvers who have situational awareness.

CENTER OPERATIONS

The Center has been chartered at the University Provost level, facilitating interdisciplinary and cross-campus collaboration. Plans have been developed for continued growth and expansion. The following principles are incorporated into the Center to ensure there is maximum learning for students that will prepare them to be successful in their chosen career pathway once graduated.

Multidisciplinary Approach

The Center actively exercises a multi-disciplinary approach to educational and research programs offered across all three campuses to both technical and non- technical students alike. An example of an educational program is our recently created Tri-Campus IA Option that leverages the strengths of all three campuses' IA course inventory. Students are allowed to choose different electives at any campus to build curriculum corresponding to any of the specialties defined by NICE [21].

All three campuses working together on a unified concentration provide a greater opportunity for students attending one campus to learn from faculty across all three campuses. This flexibility gives students the ability to customize their learning in line with their career goals. It also is much more efficient than each campus building its own program. Some courses may be offered online or in a hybrid format to encourage enrollment from distant campuses.

The Center's research agenda has evolved within the context of the ARC initiative at the Pacific Northwest National Laboratory with faculty exchanges, internship and financial support to the Center, as well as joint grants. Similar collaborative partnerships are evolving with other institutions: University of Hawaii Manoa, Aberyswyth University Wales, Interpares IV funded by the Canadian government at University of British Columbia, and Fraunhofer SIT at Darmstadt, Germany.

Participation in the Practice of IA

The University's Chief Information Security Officer, Kirk Bailey[2] presides over information assurance policies and practices across the institution and also collaborates with the academic and research programs of the Center. As an example, students annually perform penetration tests on the campus network as part of classroom assignments.

---

[2] Mr. Bailey has been featured frequently in *Information Security* magazine, which reaches 68,000 security practitioners around the world [22].

Mr. Bailey's extensive network of IA professionals, the Agora, convenes quarterly at the Seattle campus, providing educational and networking opportunities for students. Incorporating these meetings into course schedules and having members of his network make guest lecture appearances in the classroom are ways the Center integrates IA industry expertise into curricula.

Students also participate in PRISEM, our Public Regional Information Security Event Management system. This is a regional alert system that integrates and analyzes netflow data from local municipalities, ports, hospitals and local businesses to give us a sense of the regional threat patterns which inform security professionals and provide an escalation path to national and regional authorities.

Partnerships in IA Education

The CIAC is partnering on projects with several institutions of higher learning which exposes students to other universities and institutions and expands their understanding of the field. Some examples:

1) The United States Military Academy at West Point collaboration led to development of the Pacific Rim Collegiate Cyber Defense Competition (PRCCDC). This event gives students live-fire hands-on experience that simulates real world management of actual networks. The project received regional and national funding from local business and the National Collegiate Cyber Defense Competition.

2) George Washington University and University of Hawaii Manoa collaboration on an NSF grant, Sea to Shining Sea [DUE - 1128989], provided access to Washington DC IA experts through guest lecture videos and live chat.

3) Whatcom Community College-led NSF grant [*NSF Proposal #7252472*] that is developing articulation agreements with Washington State universities. At UW, it includes articulation to a Tri-Campus IA degree program.

4) Highline Community College, Seattle University and University of Washington collaboration [DUE0341356] developed Computer Forensics curriculum that has been implemented throughout the CIAC network.

5) The University of Hawaii at Manoa collaboration for IA curriculum dissemination, teaching exchange and research collaboration was funded by NSA [H98230-07-1-0244].

Each of these collaborations has leveraged and extended IA programs at the University of Washington, promoting a rich exchange of ideas and further collaborative opportunities with other university partners.

Academic Concentrations in IA

Academic concentrations in Information Assurance have been developed in multiple programs, creating a curriculum database that facilitates the ability to develop new curricula for different disciplines, as requested. Most recently, these artifacts contributed to a Master in Cyber Leadership (MCL) degree that integrates both the computer science/cybersecurity and business departments in a jointly offered degree directed toward transitioning military personnel. Approximately 8,000 veterans a year for the foreseeable future are expected to pass through military installations near the UW Tacoma campus as they transition into civilian careers.

The University is committed to accommodate the academic needs of transitioning and active military by not only offering specific programs designed for military personnel, but also by developing a database of all local cybersecurity program offerings throughout the State so service people are able to find academic programs most aligned with their needs, capabilities and interests. Called CREATES, Cybersecurity Rapid Education Apprenticeship Training Employment System, this is a pipeline from military through academia to civilian jobs. Work began on CREATES (Figure 7) during a 2010 NSF grant called *VetsEngr* [EEC 1037814].

In addition, special topics courses are developed as needed. For example, Dr. Edward Lazowska, the Bill and Melinda Gates Endowed Chair in

Computer Science and Engineering, developed and delivered a course, "Homeland Security / Cyber Security," that was a 4-site, distance-learning collaboration among the University of Washington Dept. Engineering), and Dr. Geoff Voelker (UCSD Computer Science & Engineering), UC Berkeley, UC San Diego, and Microsoft [23]. Lead instructors included Dr. Lazowska, Dr, Christine Hartmann-Siantar, Dr. Steve Maurer (UCB Goldman School of Public Policy), Dr. Stefan Savage (UCSD Computer Science).

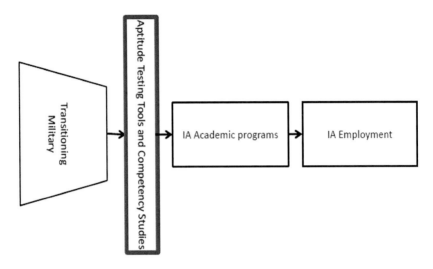

Figure 7 CREATES Pipeline

Faculty members have received national and international recognition for their research in information assurance. For example: Dr. Tadayoshi Kohno, Dr. Radha Poovendran and Dr. Barbara Endicott-Popovsky are internationally recognized leaders in computer science, electrical engineering, forensic readiness, respectively. Neal Koblitz, co-inventor of elliptic curve cryptography, offers courses in number theory and other topics and guest lectures in our IA classes.

Student Participation in Research and Publications

Our researchers expose students to the most recent developments in IA. Students are expected to publish and participate in research, regardless of level (bachelor, master, or doctorate). Student capstone projects, in partnership with industry, are reviewed in a day of research presentations at each campus for each program where students share the results of their work with faculty and peers. Some examples:

Dr. Poovendran, Professor and Chair of Electrical Engineering, is Director of Research for the Center. He embodies the Center's principle of bringing research into the classroom. He publishes extensively in wireless security and applied cryptography, and was named a Presidential Early Career Awards recipient.[3]

Dr. Tadayoshi Kohno, Associate Professor of Computer Science and Engineering, is known for his riveting research experiments that attract students, such as hacking into traveling cars, that has gained world attention.

Dr. Barbara Endicott-Popovsky, Professor UW Institute of Technology, Tacoma, who explores forensic readiness, has attracted broad interest from the international community as evidenced by her leadership at a Dagstuhl conference, Germany, attended by researchers from four continents and eleven countries, resulting in a research manifesto for forensic readiness and digit evidence. She brings students into her international collaborations.

---

[3] The highest honor bestowed by the Federal government to young researchers at the outset of their careers in technical fields.

Access to Leading Practitioners

iSchool/IA Cohorts

Cohort	Academic Year	Certificate Students (female)	Matriculated Students (female)
I	2005	11	
II	2005-6	16 (5)	
III	2006-7	18	
IV	2007-9	19 (4)	16 (4)
V	2008-9	17 (5)	8 (3)
VI	2009-10	12 (4)	14 (4)
VII	2010-11	22* (5)	30* (8) (5 WNG)
VIII	2011-12	27 (5)	33 (12) (6 WNG)
IX	2012-13	28 (6)	34(9) (2 WNG)
X	2013-14	20 (4)	22(5) (1 WNG)
		190 (29)	157 (46)

40 more next year! 50,000 in Coursera

Figure 8 Cohorts of ISRM Certificate Graduates

An example of our use of practitioners in academic programs is our Information Security and Risk Management (ISRM) certificate program developed by Dr. Endicott-Popovsky in collaboration with members of the regional IA community. The program teaches an interdisciplinary systems approach to establishing, managing, and operating a comprehensive IA program in organizations and makes ample use of practitioner guest lecturers who provide a practical perspective on topics covered in the program. The ISRM certificate is now in its 11th year and is offered in either asynchronous hybrid mode or through a MOOC (Massively Open Online Course). Over 300 students have gone through the classroom version of this program to date and many are now in leadership roles in cybersecurity.

Participants from industry who guest lecture in the program include such luminaries as:

75

1) Kirk Bailey, VP and CISO of the University of Washington,

2) Mike Hamilton, former CISO City of Seattle, founder of both MK Hamilton and Associates and PRISEM, and policy advisor to the CIO of the State of Washington,

3) Michael Simon, nationally-known network design engineer, entrepreneur and author, and now adjunct instructor in our IA programs,

4) Ilanko Subramaniam, VP Global Business Associates and national/international expert in GRC (Governance, Risk Management and Compliance), and adjunct instructor in our IA programs,

5) Seth Shapiro, VP and risk management consultant, Kibble and Prentice, who pioneered development of products that insure against cyber intrusion, also an adjunct instructor in risk management,

6) Steven Schroeder, JD, retired Federal Prosecutor who successfully prosecuted the Gorschkov case, [24]

7) William Nelson, author, teacher and Senior Digital Forensic investigator for The Boeing Company.

Involving the IA community in the program ensures that students are exposed not only to the theoretical foundation of IA and recent research in the field, but also to practitioners who are solving complex problems. The certificate culminates in a practicum that includes actual case experiences drawn from industry, a hands-on attack-defend laboratory with PRISEM and the PRCCDC, and a practical problem that students are invited to solve in collaboration with IA experts from industry. In 2014, University of Washington was ranked the 10th best place for studying cybersecurity in the country by Ponemon Institute for its outcomes-based programs [25].

USAR Cyber Public Private Initiative (P3i) Pilot Program at UW CIAC

US Army Reserve future Cyber initiatives partner directly with UW CIAC in a public-private partnership that increases advanced cyber and IA educational opportunities for Cyber Security soldiers. These educational offerings directly relate to their Cyber positions, duties and KSA development. An example of the urgent need is the Army Reserve Cyber Operations Group transition to 10 Cyber Protection Teams (390 soldiers). This transition enhances and builds a new Army cyber force structure; of which the transition of the ARGOG from 308 soldiers to around 561 soldiers is an instance.

The USAR needed a way to provide continuous education, development and advancement of apprentice and master cyber defense soldiers. The CIAC program with its broad cyber academic and technical program offerings, for resident and distance learning students at three different UW campuses links directly to 3-5 year Army Force Cyber Generation model for skills development. A UW CIAC program, such as UW Tacoma's Master in Cyber Leader (MCL), are matched to USAR Cyber leader skill development and KSAs.

Advanced USAR cyber technical positions, likewise, are matched with more technical cyber degrees such as UW Bothell's software and hardware security engineering programs.

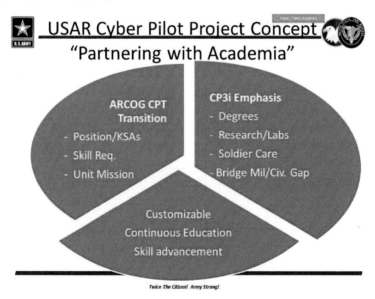

Figure 9 USAR Partnering with Academia

In other words, in the context of our partnership, a CIAC program is directly matched with a USAR Cyber soldier's position and required skill development. After a 3-4 year academic commitment, that soldier will be available for mobilization, having earned a Cyber/IA bachelors, masters or PhD. The CIAC partnership also addresses a gap in methods, tools, TTP (tactics techniques and procedures) and applied research for USAR cyber security units. Our broad partnership includes developing laboratories that provide opportunities for soldiers and students to exercise and research a broad area of cyber security and defense issues impacting industry, government and military operations.

Finally, the CIAC and USAR partnership indirectly bridges a military, industry and public sector gap as citizen soldiers' interact and are employed in civilian positions that directly apply the skills and education from UW degrees in full-time civilian and part-time military careers. At the same time, the Army and DoD gain highly skilled soldiers in support of operational military missions when on annual training, exercises or mobilized for active duty cyber defense deployments CONUS or OCONUS.

Outreach and Online Offerings

The Center has an active outreach program and has developed online educational offerings to reach students anywhere in the world. This is especially helpful for military students subject to deployment. In the last few years, we have had students participate from the mountains of Afghanistan, on navy vessels and in undisclosed areas that still have network access. We offer complete degree programs in this mode, such as our Master of Infrastructure Planning and Management (MIPM) developed, in partnership with the Washington State National Guard, the Department of Urban Design and Planning and Professional and Continuing Education at the University.

Additionally our flagship education offering, the ISRM certificate, is offered in a hybrid mode, in class and online simultaneously. In addition, the Center, in advisory collaboration with the Pacific Northwest National Labs and Battelle, has presented a public televised lecture series in Information Assurance.

CIAC continues to pursue online offerings like its MOOC being offered through Coursera:

https://www.coursera.org/course/inforiskman.

In the last three years, over 50,000 students worldwide have finished our MOOC offerings. Several have gone on to take certificate or degree programs through the university.

CONCLUSIONS AND FUTURE WORK OF THE CIAC

Through its collaborations, the Center provides significant mutual benefits for industry, the community and other academic institutions. Additionally, our leading, multidisciplinary, IA experts are available to industry and government to develop and implement advanced solutions to complex, real-world IA problems. This creates a unique environment for rich IA educational and research offerings that attract top talent, including leading faculty and highly motivated students with career and research interests in IA and cybersecurity. This has a stimulating effect on entrepreneurial efforts and innovation that attracts industry and jobs to the region, provides support to regional government for disaster preparedness related to a catastrophic cyber event, and keeps IA professionals on the cutting edge of the discipline, ensuring their competitiveness and the competitiveness of the State.

Over the next three years, the Center will continue to expand its research agenda and its academic programs, bringing together the rich individual and organizational IA talent in the Pacific Northwest. The intent is to facilitate solutions to difficult IA and cybersecurity problems.

Phase 1 -

Expand partnerships: 1) with Pacific Northwest National Laboratory (PNNL) to integrate research programs, building a wider bridge between the two institutions. The Executive Director of the Center is currently partially funded by PNNL which is enhancing the development of the partnership; 2) with Fraunhofer which unites CIAC and Fraunhofer SIT in solving forensic readiness and digital evidence issues; 3) with USAR and the State's National

Guard that extends our offerings to current and transitioning military students and assists with ramp up in cybersecurity preparedness of our military and the translation to the civilian world for those leaving military service; 4) with its array of academic, industry and government partners who will provide increased opportunities for learning and careers in IA.

Phase 2 -

During the second phase, the Center will evolve from as an increasingly significant presence nationally with its industry/private sector focus that makes the Center uniquely posed to provide a critical infrastructure perspective on IA that includes the cloud which is forming in the Northwest. This is an orientation that is an important presence in the formation of IA policy and approaches to protecting the homeland.

Phase 3 -

During the third phase, the Center will consolidate its gains and continue to expand in influence and impact. Near term projects include (1) creation of an interdisciplinary, policy-focused, research agenda to integrate the contributions of key researchers involved with the Center, 2) developing a governance model for an expanded Center that has grown and matured in the last decade (3) formalization of CREATES that includes offering cooperative opportunities to learn in the real world, (4) development of technical academic programs with increasing depth, integrated with PRISEM [26] and (5) holding more community security and awareness events as part of our outreach mission [27]

The spectrum of these efforts is directed at public and private organizations/agencies, military, different government levels (local, state, regional and Federal), across a range of other sectors: law and law enforcement, industry, academia, etc. Cyber by its nature is the connective tissue of organizations and the backbone for the flow of information and good decisions. Without identification, detection, protection, response, and recovery it will fail. This connective tissue will only become more dense, complex and critical as the internet of things provides demand, convenience and vulnerability.

REFERENCES

[1] National Security Agency. (No Date) IA Academic Outreach: NIETP. Retrieved July 12, 2014 from the World Wide Web: http://www.nsa.gov/ia/academic_outreach/index.shtml

[2] Gates, W. "Trustworthy Computing," Memo published January 15, 2002. Microsoft Corporation, Seattle, WA.

[3] Kuzmina, U. *Fundamentals of Pedagogy of Higher Education*. (Leningrad, RU: Lenizdat, 1972).

[4] Bespalko, V. *Fundamentals of Theory of Pedagogical Systems*. (Vorenege, RU: Voronege State University Press, 1977).

[5] Talizina, N.F. (1975). Management of the Learning Process. Moscow, Russia.

[6] Roginsky, V.M. (1990). Alphabet of Pedagogical Work. Moscow, Russia: School of Higher Education.

[7] Hutton, G. "Backward curriculum Design Process" Retrieved May 1, 2003 from the World Wide Web: http://www.g4v.com/~glen.hutton/ED3601/BackwardDesi gnFeb11_03.pdf

[8] Bloom, B.S., Mesia, B.B. and Krathwohl, D.R. (1964). Taxonomy of Educational Objectives. New York: David McKay.

[9] Michailova, A.F. (1985). *Establishing a system of professional–practical activity*. Moscow, Russia: Messenger of Higher Education, No. 11, pp. 31-33.

[10] Talizina, N. F. (1986). *Activity Approach to the Development of the Model Specialist*. Moscow, Russia: Messenger of Higher Education, No 3, pp. 10-14.

[11] Endicott-Popovsky, B.E. and Frincke, D., (2003, June). *A Case Study In Rapid Introduction of Computer Security Curricula*, in Proceedings from the Seventh Colloquium for Information Systems Security Education 7-10, June 2004, Washington, D.C.

[12] Endicott-Popovsky, B.E. and Frincke, D., (2004, March). *A Case Study in Rapid Introduction of a Computer Security Track into a Software Engineering Curriculum*, in Proceedings of IEEE Computer Society Press 17th Conference on Software Engineering Education and Training 1-3 March 2004, Norfolk, VA, pp. 118-123.

[13] Endicott-Popovsky, B.E., Frincke, D., Popovsky, V.M. *Designing a Computer Forensics Course for an Information Assurance Track*, in Proceedings from the Eighth Colloquium for Information Systems Security Education 7-10, June 2004, United States Military Academy, West Point, NY, pp.59-64.

[14] Endicott-Popovsky, B.E., Taylor, C., Popovsky, V.M., (2005, February). *International Curriculum Design for Undergraduate Computer Science*, in Proceedings of SIGCSE Technical Symposium on Computer Science Education.

[15] Endicott-Popovsky, B.E., Frincke, D., Popovsky, V.M., (2005, June). *Secure Code: The Capstone Class in an IA Track*, in Proceedings from the Ninth Colloquium for Information Systems Security Education 6-9, June 2005, Georgia Institute of Technology, Atlanta, GA, pp.100-108.

[16] Popovsky, V.M., Endicott-Popovsky, B.E., *Physical Culture Pedagogy: Coaching by Design*, V.E. Grigoriev (Ed.). (2005) Methods for Modernizing Physical Culture: Selection of Scientific and Methodological Works, St. Petersburg, Russia, pp. 176-187.

[17] Endicott-Popovsky, B.E., Seifert, C. Frincke, D. *Adopting Extreme Programming on a Graduate Student Project*, in Proceedings from the Sixth IEEE Systems, Man and Cybernetics Information Assurance Workshop 15-17 June 2005, United States Military Academy, West Point, NY, pp.454-455.

[18] Popovsky, V.M. (1988) *The System of Continuous Pedagogical Practice in IPC*. S.P Evseev and V.M. Popovsky(Ed.) Organization and Methodology of Continuous Pedagogical Practicums in the Institute of Physical Culture: Academic Methodological Benefits, Leningrad: Lesgaft Institute of Physical Culture.

[19] Ageevec, V.U., Popovsky, V.M., Filippov, S.S. (1984) *The Mini–Department of the Institute of Physical Culture–A New Form Of Student Work*. Theory and Practice of Physical Culture, Moscow: Russia, No 11.

[20] *Networks: A Post Mortem*, in Proceedings of the Safety and Security in a Networked World: Balancing Cyber- Rights & Responsibilities Conference at the Oxford Internet Institute, The University of Oxford, Oxford, England. Retrieved September 9, 2005 from the World Wide Web: http://www.oii.ox.ac.uk/research/cybersafety/?view=papers

[21] National Academies of Science. Rising above the Gathering Storm: *Energizing and Employing America for a Brighter Economic Future*. (Washington, D.C.: The National Academies Press, 2005).

[22] Endicott-Popovsky, B.E., Orton, I., Bailey, K. Frincke, D. *Community Security Awareness Training*, in Proceedings from the Sixth IEEE Systems, Man and Cybernetics Information Assurance Workshop 15-17 June 2005, United States Military Academy, West Point, NY, pp.373-379.

[23] Endicott-Popovsky, B. and Popovsky, V. (2013). Application of pedagogical fundamentals for the holistic development of cybersecurity professionals. *ACM Inroads, Cybersecurity Edition, March 2014.*

[24] NIST/NICE framework http://csrc.nist.gov/nice/framework/

[25] Sherman, E. *Peer to Peer*. (2005, January) In <u>Information Security</u>, Retrieved March 18, 2006 from the World Wide Web: http://informationsecurity.techtarget.com/magItem/0,2912 66,sid42_gci1042652,00.html

[26] Hartmann-Siantar, C, Lazowska, E., Maurer, S., Savage, S., and Voelker G. (2005, Autumn). <u>CSE P 590TU: Homeland Security / Cyber Security</u>. Retrieved March 18, 2006 from the World Wide Web: http://www.cs.washington.edu/education/courses/csep590/05au/

[27] Endicott-Popovsky, B.E., Ryan, D., Frincke, D. (2005, September). *The New Zealand Hacker Case: Tracking Down a Vengeful Hacker Through Public Networks: A Post Mortem*, in <u>Proceedings of the Safety and Security in a Networked World: Balancing Cyber- Rights & Responsibilities Conference at the Oxford Internet Institute</u>, The University of Oxford, Oxford, England. Retrieved September 9, 2005 from the World Wide Web: http://www.oii.ox.ac.uk/research/cybersafety/?view=papers

[28] Ponemon Institute, 2014 Best Schools for Cybersecurity Report. Retrieved at: http://www.ponemon.org/library/2014-best-schools-for-cybersecurity

[29] National Academies of Science. *Rising above the Gathering Storm: Energizing and Employing America for a Brighter Economic Future*. (Washington, D.C.: The National Academies Press, 2005).

[30] Endicott-Popovsky, B.E., Orton, I., Bailey, K. Frincke, D. *Community Security Awareness Training*, in <u>Proceedings from the Sixth IEEE Systems, Man and Cybernetics Information Assurance Workshop 15-17 June 2005</u>, United States Military Academy, West Point, NY, pp.373-379.

Easing Student Veterans' Transition to Cybersecurity and STEM through a "Math Boot Camp"

Helen Burn, Ph.D.
Department of Mathematics
Highline College

Michael Mulcahy, Ph.D.
Department of Sociology
Central Washington University – Des Moines

Barbara Endicott-Popovsky, Ph.D.
School of Information
University of Washington

Abstract - In this paper, we report on data collected from a group of student veterans who participated in a community college "Math Boot Camp" for student veterans interested in Cybersecurity and STEM fields. The Math Boot Camp combined three levels of remedial mathematics into a single course that relied heavily on interactive, instructional software. The strategic importance of remedial math classes results from the confluence of three factors: the importance of math skills in STEM degrees; veterans' interest in STEM fields; and veterans' actual and/or perceived math skill deficits. We describe the Math Boot Camp and present pre- and post-survey and focus group data collected from the 17 participants. The findings revealed that student veterans entered the Math Boot Camp with a positive view of the importance of mathematics to their lives and were not overly anxious about the course. Fifteen of seventeen students passed the course (2.0 or above). In focus groups, the student veterans commented most frequently about the positive benefits of instructor and the class tutor, the hybrid nature of the course, and the flexibility of placement and advancement afforded by the multi-level classroom. We present implications for design and evaluation of transition courses for student veterans in STEM and policy implication related to Post-9/11 GI bill benefits.

INTRODUCTION

Over 754,000 veterans and their families have used Post-9/11 GI Bill benefits since the law was enacted in 2008 (National Center for Veterans Analysis and Statistics, 2015). Among this student population, public two-year institutions (henceforth: 'community colleges') are a common starting point for their post-service educational career. Furthermore, student veterans beginning their postsecondary education at community colleges have been consistently more likely (than non-veterans peers) to pursue a degree in a STEM field (Science, Technology, Engineering and Mathematics; U.S. Department of Education, n.d.). On the other hand, veterans face academic and social challenges in transitioning from military to college that result in lower retention and attainment rates for this group. Barriers to veteran students' educational success can be eased, however, through transition courses that integrate student veterans into college culture and establish a peer community while focusing on core academic topics. In this paper, we report on the experiences and outcomes of student veterans enrolled in one such course - a community college "Math Boot Camp" for veterans interested in Cybersecurity and STEM fields.

The thesis guiding the development of the Veterans' Math Boot Camp was that remedial math classes offer a particularly important opportunity to facilitate veterans' social and academic integration in community college, and increase the likelihood of their success in attaining a STEM-related postsecondary degree. The strategic importance of remedial math classes results from the confluence of three factors: the importance of math skills in STEM degrees; veterans' interest in STEM fields; and veterans' actual and/or perceived math skill deficits. We discuss the project and the data in the context of recent research on veterans' transition to college. Given the national need to cultivate STEM talent (NSF, 2012; PCAST, 2012), this paper should interest faculty and administrators responsible for creating programs for student veterans in STEM.

RELEVANT LITERATURE

Student Veterans' Enrollment Patterns in Community Colleges

For decades, public two-year institutions served as the primary portal to postsecondary education for student military veterans. Data from the National Postsecondary Student Aid Studies revealed that 52.7% of veterans who began their postsecondary education in the 1995-96 academic year started out at community colleges (U.S. Department of Education, n.d.). The percentage grew to 56.2% in 1999-2000 and to about 66% in 2003-04 before beginning a decline to only 39.5% in 2011. The decrease in community college enrollments among new student veterans in the second half of the last decade was largely due to the growing role of for-profit postsecondary education businesses in this period, which accounted for about 37.5% of the 2011-12 cohort of new student veteran enrollments. For the better part of the last two decades, then, community colleges have been the preferred starting point for military veterans beginning their postsecondary education, although for-profit businesses have begun to contest the dominance of community colleges in recent years.

Indeed, not only are veterans more likely than their non-veteran peers to start their postsecondary education at community colleges, but veterans at community colleges are more likely than non-veterans to choose a STEM field. In fact, many community colleges now offer four-year bachelor of applied science [BAS] degrees in fields including IT and computer science. In the most recent NPSAS survey (2011-12), 23.8% of veterans enrolled in community colleges were in a STEM related field, compared to 15.5% of non-veterans. Furthermore, data from the *Baccalaureate and Beyond 2008* study show veterans who attained a Bachelor's degree in a STEM field in 2008 were more than twice as likely as non-veterans to have started at a community college (26.4% of veterans vs. 11.5% of non-veterans, t= -1.94).

Student Veterans' Transition to Higher Education

Recent research documents a host of challenges students veterans face as they transition to higher education. Academically, studies have found that student veterans report the subjective feeling that they are "behind" their non-veteran peers; student veterans talk about the need to "catch up," academically, to their non-veteran peers. They report that their academic preparation is deficient, particularly in mathematics, and that they have weak study skills or lack of focus, sometimes associated with PTSD (DiRamio, Ackerman, & Mitchell, 2008). Students who redeploy report academic setbacks such as needing to repeat a prerequisite mathematics course taken previously (Rumann & Hamrick, 2010). Socially, student veterans are challenged by role incongruities between civilian and military life and by the loose structure of college life. Student veterans report that differences in maturity levels interfere with developing relationships with their civilian student peers. While this is due in part to factors such as age and family responsibilities, student veterans also report that their military experience intensified their belief in the importance of educational attainment and heightened their cultural awareness, separating them from their civilian peers (DiRamio et al., 2008; DiRamio & Jarvis, 2011; Persky, 2010; Rumann & Hamrick, 2010).

Furthermore, in interaction with other students, faculty and staff, student veterans frequently encounter ignorance and lack of understanding of the military, military veterans, and their experiences, as well as negative attitudes and stereotypes. These experiences alienate student veterans, withhold needed validation of an important dimension of their identity, and thus hinder their transition and the incorporation of "student" as an identity dimension (DiRamio et al., 2008; Rumann & Hamrick, 2010). With respect to faculty relationships in particular – a point to which we return in our discussion of the Math Boot Camp below – students report both positive and negative experiences – finding very supportive faculty, as well as instructors who use their control of classroom interaction to derogate the military and military service and create a hostile environment for student veterans. As DiRamio et al. (2008) point out, it is not that student veterans desire special status; instead,

87

they wish that faculty would "understand and acknowledge them" (p. 95), and appreciate their life circumstances.

To help student veterans transition to college, DiRamio and Jarvis (2011) recommend that colleges develop transition courses to improve academic performance, and co-curricular activities (e.g., orientations) that promoting peer-group interactions. The Math Boot Camp was designed to accomplish the necessary academic skills remediation and, at the same time, address social, cultural and logistic challenges that student veterans face during the transition to postsecondary education. This focus on academic and social integration is consistent with Tinto's (1975, 1993, 2004) integration framework, which posits that students who develop a more complex network of relationships with the institution, academically and socially, are less likely to drop out, especially in the first year. In commuter schools such as community colleges, the classroom environment is instrumental in fostering academic integration. However, while it is well-established that interactions with peer groups and faculty positively influence students outcomes in college (Pascarella & Terenzini, 2005), research is not yet clear about whether a "segregated" or "cohort" strategy hinders opportunities for student veterans to integrate into the larger campus and to establish relationship with civilian peer students (DiRamio & Jarvis, 2011).

Student Veterans' Math Readiness

The mathematics required for STEM degrees can range from introductory statistics to graduate level mathematics (Klappenberger, 2014). Student veterans interested in STEM fields but with insufficient mathematics preparation will be required to complete remedial mathematics courses. The challenge this presents for student veterans cannot be overstated. On the one hand, students who successfully complete remedial mathematics courses obtain college degrees at similar rates to students who arrive "college-ready" in mathematics (Bahr, 2010; Bettinger & Long, 2005). More than half of students referred to remedial courses, however, never enroll in them, or enroll but do not complete or do not pass the class (Attewell, Lavin, Domina, & Levey, 2006; Cullinane & Treisman, 2010).

Data from the NPSAS allows us to form some snapshots – albeit coarse and grainy – with regard to questions of community college student veterans' math readiness and participation in remedial academic courses. For example, in the 2011-12 NPSAS survey, student veterans at community colleges at the time of the survey had average math SAT scores of 489.4, compared to 476.5 for non-veterans (t = 1.29). Among community college STEM majors however, veterans' average math SAT score was 482.2, compared to 496.0 for non-veterans (t = -.74). Among current community college students in their first or second year of studies, veterans were more likely to take a remedial math class in the survey year, compared to their non-veteran counterparts (9.1% vs. 7%, t = .81), and 12.9% of community college student veterans in STEM fields took a remedial math class in the 2011-12 academic year, compared to only 7% of non-veterans.

METHODS

Data for this study derived from 17 military veteran students who participated in a "Math Boot Camp" at a community college in Washington State in 2011. Another group of student veterans completed a Math Boot Camp in the summer of 2012. Our analysis focuses on the data from the 2011 cohort completed by researchers at the University of Washington which included pre and post-course survey (n=16 and n= 12, respectively; on four pre-post matched questions, n=10 for one question, and 11 for the remaining three), focus group data (n=10, 30% female, 70% male, 40% underrepresented minorities), and student persistence and achievement data. IRB was secured through the University of Washington.[1] The surveys included demographic information, Likert scale items about attitudes towards mathematics and academics, and several open-response questions about students' goals, and perceived barriers and challenges to reaching those goals. In focus groups held during the final week of class, the course participants shared their experiences in the course, discussed the aspects that they found most helpful, and offered suggestions for improvement.

---

[1] We are grateful to Dr. Liz Moore who served as evaluator for the VetsEngrProject grant and designed and conducted all surveys and focus groups.

Below, we present analyses of these data – descriptive statistics and analyses of pre-post changes, as measured by Wilcoxon signed-rank tests.[2] The open-response survey questions and focus group data were coded for themes using HyperRESEARCH™ software. Given the small sample size, the analyses are descriptive and interpretative, and intended to identify themes and compare the participants' pre-entry characteristics, academic outcomes, attitudes, feelings and expectations regarding math and their educational and career goals, impressions of the boot camp, and pre-post attitudinal changes.

MATH BOOT CAMP DESCRIPTION

The Math Boot Camp offered at Highline College [HC] was part of the VetsEngrProject (NSF 1037814, 2010-2012) secured by the University of Washington's Center for Information Assurance and Cybersecurity (CIAC). The purpose of the VetsEngrProject was to identify and overcome challenges military service members face in using their educational benefits, especially in pursuit of science, technology, engineering, and math [STEM] careers. Highline College was selected to host the boot camp due to its mathematics curriculum and location in the Puget Sound Region, 30 minutes from Joint Base Lewis McChord and Camp Murray, which services Washington National Guard (NGWA). The Math Boot Camp took place during an 8-week summer quarter in 2011 at HC campus (June 20 through August 10), and was taught by the lead author. Two classes were offered daily, and course participants were military veterans, members of the Washington National Guard, and reservists. Cohort recruiting was accomplished through NGWA Employment Transition Services team, HCC, veteran's organizations, and word of mouth[3].

The Math Boot Camp combined three levels of precollege mathematics (Math 81, 91, 98)[4] into a single course, using the Emporium Model (NCAT, 2005). The Emporium Model relies heavily on interactive instructional

---

[2] Wilcoxon sign-rank tests can be used when sample sizes are small, and assumptions of normality are violated.
[3] We are grateful to Morgan Zantua for help in recruiting and advising the participants.
[4] The three courses were Introduction to Algebra (Math 81), Essentials of Intermediate Algebra (Math 91), and Intermediate Algebra for Calculus (Math 98). Curriculum guides, including course content, are available upon request from the lead author.

software, and thus requires a computer-equipped classroom. The Math Boot Camp used MyMathLab[5] software that included online videos, worked examples, homework problems, and online quizzes. The use of these tools allowed students to set their own pace as they work through material. At the same time, the Emporium model is intended to reduce the proportion of face-to-face time consumed in one-way instructor-to-student communication. Instead of lecturing, instructional staff circulate among students, interacting and responding directly to the questions and needs of individuals or small groups.

The Math Boot Camp was offered as a hybrid course, to take full advantage of the flexibility built into the Emporium model – the online component permitted student veterans to keep up if they were unable to physically attend classes. To accommodate the multi-level structure, all of the participants were registered for "Math 80" and then self-determined their initial placement (Math 81, 91, or 98) on the first day of class, by working through sets of level-specific sample problems. At the end of the quarter, student veterans received credit either for Math 81, Math 91, or Math 98, depending on how far they had progressed over the summer. Of the 17 Math Boot Camp participants, seven initially placed themselves in Math 81, another seven placed themselves in Math 91, and three began working at the level of Math 98. In most cases, the student veterans chose the appropriate level for themselves, though a few subsequently decided to drop back a level and proceed at a slower pace.

The Math Boot Camp met daily, Monday through Thursday, for 80 minutes in a computer classroom, with an instructor and a tutor present at all times. Despite the multi-level nature of the course, it convened as a single, math level-integrated section. Student veterans were provided a highly detailed syllabus that included a pacing and timeline schedule for each of the three levels, as well as homework and quiz due dates. There were two exams, and a comprehensive final exam on the last day. Five of the participants took advantage of a two-week extension of the final exam due date, which was introduced to accommodate student veterans who missed the initial final exam

---

[5] MyMathLab is a Pearson Education product
 (http://www.pearsonmylabandmastering.com/northamerica/mymathlab/)

date due to service obligations. The design of the course allowed student veterans to work independently, in groups, or with the help of the instructor and tutor. The multi-level format allowed student veterans to learn at their own pace and, if necessary, dip back into an earlier level to fill a specific knowledge gap, without having to complete the entire earlier course. The instructor monitored progress with daily check-ins, and level-specific group instruction once or twice a week. On a typical day, seven student veterans were present in a given class.

Several class sessions included teaching study skills and building students' academic identity. The student veterans were thus provided with tools such as mechanical pencils, erasers, note cards, bus passes, and folders to organize their work, i.e., functional but also symbolically meaningful "tools of the trade" – material elements of the new institutional culture. In one class session, students viewed and discussed a video about *growth mindset* (Dweck, 2006) and were introduced to the argument that beliefs about the malleability of intelligence (e.g., having either a growth or fixed mindset) can influence long-term achievement and persistence. Students also received in-class advising by the instructor. Dr. Endicott-Popovsky from the University of Washington visited the class as well, to discuss pathways to careers in cybersecurity. The grant covered all costs, including tuition, text books, calculators and other supplies that were provided to the student veterans.

FINDINGS

This section begins with key student pre-entry characteristics identified in the "pre-treatment" survey: demographics, educational and career goals, and attitudes towards math. Following this, we present the data on student achievement, student impressions of the Math Boot Camp drawn from the focus groups and, finally, pre-post survey changes in student attitudes.

Student Pre-Entry Characteristics

Demographics

A total of 17 student veterans enrolled in the course (37% female; 63% male). Two additional participants were spouses or relatives of student veterans, and were omitted from the analysis. The student veterans ranged from 22 to 64 years of age, with an average age of 39. Participants were racially diverse: 20% African-American/Black, 7% Hispanic/Latino, 6% Asian/Pacific Islander, 7% Native American/Alaska native, and 60% Caucasian/white. The modal service branch affiliation was the Army (53%) followed by the Navy (20%), the Marines (13%), and the Air Force (13%). Nine (60%) identified their status as "veterans," "inactive," or "retired." Four (27%) identified as currently serving in the National Guard, or Reserves. The participants' length of service ranged from two to 20 years, with an average of eight years and two months.

Educational and career goals

Thirteen student veterans responded to pre-survey questions about their educational and career goals, and reasons for enrolling in the Math Boot Camp. Most (69%) stated an educational goal of a bachelor's level or above: masters (4), professional/med (2), bachelors (3), AA or AAS (2), or other (2). Student veterans stated a variety of career goals: medical school (3), IT or engineering (2), "civilian job" (6), human services (1), unknown (1). Respondents chose the Boot Camp "to prep for a future math course" (5), to "build confidence" (2), to "refresh their math skills" (3), to "prepare for the GRE" (2), or because of the opportunities to accelerate (1).

Attitudes towards mathematics

Student veterans entered the Math Boot Camp with a positive view of the importance of mathematics to their lives. On pre-surveys, the vast majority (13) agreed somewhat or strongly that math is important in daily life. Twelve students agreed they needed math for their major, and ten cited mathematics as part of the *critical path* to their career goal, stating, for example, that "mathematics is an integral component of the educational degree I would like to pursue." Most (10) stated they had not adjusted their educational or career goal because of a math challenge. In an open-response question, 40% of the respondents expressed having no concerns, while the remainder stated concerns about long-term retention of learning (30%), the ability to learn mathematics (20%), and time (10%). Table 1 shows additional pre-entry questions related to attitudes towards mathematics and reveals that the Math Boot Camp participants were not overly anxious about mathematics but acknowledged the need for remediation.

Survey Question	Percent Agreed
I'm rusty in math, just need a refresher	80%
Math is very helpful for any course of study	73%
I'm willing to take more than the required mathematics classes	67%
I have a very weak math background	53%
I have low math ability	40%
I am worried about this course	36%
I prefer to avoid math in college	20%

Table 1: Pre-entry characteristics of participants (n=15) related to attitudes towards mathematics

Student Achievement in Math Boot Camp

Fifteen of seventeen (88%) of the Math Boot Camp student veterans passed their chosen course with a 2.0 or above (5/7 in Math 81, 7/7 in Math 91 and 3/3 in Math 98). One student completed both Math 91 and 98 in the quarter; and two student veterans originally started in Math 91 and dropped back to complete Math 81. At the end of the course, 10 student veterans (59%) had enrolled in a follow-on math course at HC. Of the remaining seven students, four enrolled in the Math Boot Camp for personal interest or to hone their math skills for the GRE and were not planning to enroll in further mathematics courses at HC, one was deciding which college is the best choice for their next course, one had secured employment and did not plan to attend college, and one student was undecided.

Student Impressions of Math Boot Camp

In focus groups, the student veterans commented most frequently (10) about the instructor and the class tutor. Participants emphasized the importance of personal, one-on-one contact with the instructor and the tutor (5), and noted that the instructor worked well with student veterans to make sure they understood the concepts (4). For example, one student veteran commented that, when students were having trouble, they would "…go to the whiteboard and get help one-on-one." Many student veterans contrasted this with negative experiences in previous math classes, where they felt the teacher was distant, inaccessible, or moved too fast, without worrying about whether they fell behind (5). One student described the Math Boot Camp as "more of a one-on-one" that "made a difference" for the participants, in contrast to their last math class, where "there were 20 people and once you fell behind, you were done."

Positive assessments of the hybrid structure of the course constituted the second major theme in the focus group comments (7). Participants underscored the advantages associated with having access to course materials outside of class, including being able to do homework and quizzes online. One student commented that the hybrid structure made it possible for him to accommodate a two week absence without falling behind. In this context, again, student veterans contrasted the boot camp experience with prior negative classroom experiences, which left them feeling uncomfortably aware of academic weaknesses, compared to their peers, or embarrassed about having to take remedial courses (5).

Five student veterans commented on the positive benefits of a multi-level classroom and flexibility of placement and advancement. One student is paraphrased as saying, "Multi-level is a plus. You can start where you feel you're comfortable, and if [it's] too easy or too difficult, [you] can move to a different level." Five student veterans requested that this format be used for other introductory courses. For example, one student is paraphrased as saying,

Do you have one of these for English 101? When you've been out of the educational loop for a while and you get back into college level writing, you can get hit right away with a bunch of stuff. Help out all entry level requirements to get you into college.

Lastly, three student veterans commented specifically on the benefits of the cohort model, expressed by one student who commented that the class was less intimidating because "it's for veterans" so you "don't feel as dumbed down" compared to being in a class with "kids right out of high school who did the math a year or two ago."

Attitudinal Changes Resulting from Math Boot Camp Experience

The Math Boot Camp had a positive effect on student veterans' attitudes towards mathematics, as shown in Table 2. After taking the Math Boot Camp, student veterans were less worried about the course, were less likely to believe they had low math ability, less likely to believe they had test-taking anxiety and more likely to agree that math is helpful for any major.

		Means		Sign Test[a]	Wilcoxon Signed-Rank Test[b]	
Question	N	Pre	Post	p-value	z	Prob > |z|
Worried about this class	10	2.8	3.9	0.008*	− 2.581	0.010**
Low math ability	11	2.9	3.8	0.016*	− 2.408	0.016*
Test-taking anxiety in math	11	2.5	3.3	0.062+	− 1.986	0.047*
Math is helpful for any major	11	2.1	1.4	1	1.992	0.046*

+ p<0.10; *p<0.05; **p<0.01   a: One-tailed tests

Strongly Agree = 1 – Strongly Disagree = 5   b: two-tailed tests

Table 2: Sign Tests of Matched Pre- and Post-Survey Responses

Open-response survey questions suggest that the boot camp experience may have transitioned student veterans from focusing mainly on logistical challenges associated with reaching their educational goal, to focusing more on the intellectual or academic challenges. Specifically, both pre- and post-surveys asked student veterans what they saw as the greatest challenge to achieving their educational and career goals. Six of nine student veterans with pre-survey responses cited general challenges related to school, such as "I have not been in school for a while" or challenges of a logistic nature, such as "time," "school finances," "working to pay bills while attending courses." The remaining three cited challenges related to academics, such as "retaining all the information this career field throws at you," or "understanding mathematics." It is noteworthy that this trend reversed itself on the post-surveys, where eight student veterans responded and all but one cited intellectual or academic challenges, such as "college-level math" or "finishing the required courses."

Several post-survey questions assessed the extent to which the experience of the Math Boot Camp had changed their perspectives on the challenges they face in the effort to achieve their educational goals. Seven student veterans responded that the course boosted their confidence. One student's response illustrates this pattern: "This class has significantly boosted my confidence and ability to succeed in the accomplishment of this goal." Another student veteran stated, "I have learned that it may not be as difficult as it may seem." Furthermore, none of the student veterans changed their stated career or educational goal between and pre- and post-survey, and the majority of participants continued to view mathematics as part of the critical path to achieving those goals. Indeed, when asked how, if at all, the course had affected what they see as possible career and educational goals, half the respondents stated that they now saw their career goal as more obtainable, and half expressed that they now saw math as more doable, or as less of an obstacle, or they had a better understanding about what their math options are.

DISCUSSION

The thesis guiding the development of the Veterans' Math Boot Camp was that remedial math classes offer a particularly important opportunity to facilitate veterans' transition to community college, and to increase the likelihood of their success in attaining a STEM-related postsecondary degree. The strategic importance of remedial math classes results from the confluence of three factors: the importance of math skills in STEM degrees; veterans' interest in STEM fields; and veterans' actual and/or perceived math skill deficits. This discussion focuses on implications for design and evaluation of future transition courses and policy implications related to the Post-9/11 GI bill benefits.

DiRamio and Jarvis (2011) recommend that colleges help student veterans integrate academically and socially into college by developing transition courses for student veterans to improve academic performance and co-curricular activities that promote peer-group interactions, whereby – at least in the early stages of student veterans' transition – peers are defined as other student veterans. The findings of this study suggest that transitional courses designed according to the Emporium Model (NCAT, 2005), like the Math Boot Camp described above, hold promise with regard to both of these twin goals. Segregated transitional remediation courses offer opportunities for the development of peer networks among student veterans that facilitate the initial transition; they also create a relatively "safe" environment in which student veterans can address perceived or real academic deficits; and the course structure facilitates mastery of academic material and improved academic performance by meeting the logistic needs of this student population. We believe this model could also be adapted to other core subject areas. Indeed, student veterans in our study asked for additional introductory courses patterned after the Boot Camp. Key features of the model include: academic subjects vital to students success (e.g., English, mathematics, introductory STEM courses), highly structured and interactive learning environment, high-quality instruction, flexibility in pacing scheduling, and teaching non-cognitive skills (e.g., study skills and academic identity). Particularly within area of mathematics, research reveals that helping students understand themselves as learners and providing early mastery experiences are key to building students' self-efficacy and, hence, persistence and attainment (Yeager & Dweck, 2012). Our findings regarding the importance of intense instructor contact highlights the advantage of small class size, and the need to select instructors who are willing to reach out and not only help students to master the subject matter, but also help them to learn about college, help to create positive classroom experiences, and encourage students to believe in themselves as learners - that is, instructors who *validate* students (Rendon, 1994).

The findings also have implications for program evaluation of transition courses for student veterans in STEM. For example, the goals of a successful transition course include exposing students to realistic academic experiences and expectations. While caution must be taken in interpreting our findings, given the small sample size, there was evidence that the Math Boot Camp experience shifted students' focus from primarily logistic challenges (e.g., time and money) to the intellectual challenges associated with completing college, while maintaining or even boosting student confidence. Program evaluation should including measures of student achievement but also measure the extent to which student veterans have widened their focus regarding challenges. Attention should also be given to non-cognitive outcomes, such as pre-post changes in confidence and attitudes.

Several policy issues arose in developing and delivering the Math Boot Camp – issues that we were only able to overcome because the VetsEngrProject grant covered all student costs: students participated in the Math Boot Camp without tapping their educational benefits. This enabled us to implement several organizational innovations that may be untenable under the current VA certifying guidelines. First, we purposely avoided placement testing in the Math Boot Camp and instead placed students based on a first-day activity. In general, however, student veterans are required to take a placement test to validate that they need remediation courses. Next, student veterans are not allowed to take remedial courses that are math labs or independent study. During the project, the lead author became aware that in at least one state there was a debate occurring about whether the Emporium Model constitutes a math lab. Lastly, we were advised that having student enroll initially in "Math 80" and then awarding credit for a different course (e.g., Math 81, 91, or 98) would not pass a VA audit and student veterans may be required to pay back money. These issues need to be considered in designing future transition courses of this nature.

Finally, the findings of the Math Boot Camp revealed several gaps in the literature related to student veterans' transition and persistence. For example, the Math Boot Camp research shows the perceived value to students of having a classroom comprising only student veterans – that is a "segregation" strategy. Still, given the small sample size, this is an open question that warrants continued exploration. And while most recent research has focused on social and cultural integration, future research needs to tease out the differential effects of academic versus social factors in student veterans' lower rates of persistence. For example, was the possible shift in focus from logistics to academics revealed in this study a case of unrealistic expectations or *misdirected expectations* (Alexander, Bozick, & Entwisle, 2008)? Do realistic expectations increase the likelihood of persistence? These are just a few questions unearthed by this study that warrant future research.

REFERENCES

[1] Alexander, K., R. Bozick, & D. Entwisle. (2008). Warming up, cooling out, or holding steady? Persistence and change in educational expectations after high school. *Sociology of Education* 81, 371-396.

[2] Attewell, P., Lavin, D., Domina, T., & Levey, T. (2006). New evidence on college remediation. *The Journal of Higher Education*, 77(5), 886-924.

[3] Bahr, P. R. (2010). Revisiting the efficacy of postsecondary remediation: The moderating effects of depth/breath of deficiency. *The Review of Higher Education*, 233(2), 177-205.

[4] Bettinger, E. P., & Long, B. T. (2005). Addressing the needs of under-prepared students in higher education: Does college remediation work? (NBER Working Paper No. 11325). Retrieved from National Bureau of Economic Research Website: www.nber.org/papers/w11325

[5] Cullinane, J., & Treisman, P. U. (2010). *Improving developmental mathematics education in community colleges: A prospectus and early progress report on the Statway Initiative.* Paper presented at the National Center for Postsecondary Research Conference, New York, N.Y. Retrieved from National Center for Postsecondary Research Website: http://www.postsecondaryresearch.org/conference/downloads.html

[6] DiRamio, D., Ackerman, R.A., and Mitchell, R.I. (2008). From combat to campus: Voices of student veterans. *NASPA Journal*, 45(1), 73-102.

[7] DiRamio, D., & Jarvis, K. (2011). Veterans in higher Education: When Johnny and Jane come marching to campus. *ASHE Higher Education Report*, 37(3). Hoboken, NJ: Wiley Periodicals, Inc.

[8] Dweck, C. S. (2006). *Mindset*. New York: Random House.

[9] Klappenberger, F. (2014). *A guide for mapping courses to knowledge units (KUs)*. Largo, MD: National Cyberwatch Center.

[10] The National Center for Academic Transformation. (2005). *Redesigning Mathematics: Increasing Student Success at a Reduced Cost*. Retrieved from http://www.thencat.org/RedMathematics.htm.

[11] National Center for Veterans Analysis and Statistics. (2015). *Utilization*. Retrieved from http://www.va.gov/vetdata/Utilization.asp.

[12] National Science Foundation. (2012). *Veterans' Education for Engineering and Science: Report on the National Science Foundation Workshop on Enhancing the Post-9/11 Veterans' Education Benefit*. Maclean, VA: NSF.

[13] President's Council of Advisors on Science and Technology (PCAST). (2012). *Engage to excel: Producing one million additional college graduates with degrees in science, technology, engineering, and mathematics*. Washington, DC: The White House.

[14] Pascarella, E., & Terenzini, P. (2005). *How college affects students: A third decade of research*. San Francisco, CA: Jossey-Bass

[15] Persky, K.R. (2010). *Veterans education: Coming home to the community college classroom*. Unpublished doctoral dissertation, National-Louis University. Retrieved November 16, 2012, from http://digitalcommons.nl.edu/diss/31/.

[16] Rendon, L. (1994). Validating culturally diverse students: Toward a new model *Innovative Higher Education*, 19(1), 33-51.

[17] Rumann, C. B., & Hamrick, F. A. (2010). Student veterans in transition: Re-enrolling after war zone deployments. *Journal of Higher Education*, 81(4), 431-538.

[18] Tinto, V. (1975). Dropout from higher education: A theoretical synthesis of recent research. *Review of Educational Research*, 45(1), 89-125.

[19] Tinto, V. (1993). *Leaving college: Rethinking the causes and cures of student attrition* (2nd ed.). Chicago: University of Chicago Press.

[20] Tinto, V. (2004). Linking learning and leaving. In J.M. Braxton (Ed.), *Reworking the student departure puzzle*. Nashville, TN: Vanderbilt University Press.

[21] U.S. Department of Education. Institute of Education Sciences, National Center for Education Statistics. (n.d.) *National Postsecondary Student Aid Study (NPSAS)*. Retrieved from http://nces.ed.gov/surveys/npsas/

[22] Yeager, D. S., & Dweck, C. S. (2012). Mindsets that promote resilience: When students believe that personal characteristics can be developed. *Educational Psychologist*, 47(4), 302-314.

Journey of a Veteran: Transitional Pathway from Military to Civilian IT and Cybersecurity Workforce through Educational Advancement

Tyler Stark
Roger Yin, Ph.D.
University of Wisconsin-Whitewater

The following article is a narrative recounting the experience of one veteran. We are offering this to you as representative of the voices of America's vets. This article will not increase your knowledge of the field. But it will give you practical insight into the hearts and minds of the people who you serve and who are the subject of this special edition. The opinions in this are the author's. However the insights presented belong to every member of the educational community. Please read and enjoy.

INTRODUCTION

According to a study conducted by Morin (2011) at Pew Research Center, 44% of veterans found it very to extremely difficult to transition back into the civilian workforce. The following is an in depth case study which will take you through the experience that an army veteran endured when transitioning from active duty to civilian life. The scope of this paper is to show other service members, within the IT and cybersecurity field specifically, the "best practices" in regards to choosing a university for educational advancement, identifying and obtaining proper cybersecurity skills and industry certifications, and successfully transitioning from military to civilian life.

BIG DECISION AT THE CROSSROADS

It all just seemed to hit Joe one day. Joe woke up in a cold sweat with his stomach twisted into knots as the sweat beaded off his forehead. He asked himself, "Was I sick? Did I have the flu? Did I have a bad dream?" These were questions that Joe thought would get him to the truth as to why he was in the condition that he was in. As this particular Monday morning progressed, it all started to dawn on Joe that he had joined the United States Army in October of 2010 and within the blink of an eye, his four years was almost up.

This is when the stress really started to kick in and the true worries and questions started manifesting themselves in full force. Joe remembers this particular day like it was yesterday, May 5th, 2014. This is the day that he remembers as decision day, as the two by four to the head saying, "Wake up Joe, what are you going to do now?"

When asked why he joined the service Joe had a very unique and rather different response than most fellow service members. The response was similar in that Joe felt it was his duty to serve the country, but where his response differed is that he mainly joined the military for a *Defining Life Experience*. An experience that would live in his mind for the rest of his life. An experience that would provide him with countless stories to tell his children and grandchildren. Joe wanted to make his mother and father proud, while paying the debt to this great country that we all lived and prospered in. You see, Joe believes that it is the responsibility of each and every person living in this country to serve and defend her, even if it means giving up their own lives. Like most other service members and many American people, he believes that freedom is not free but rather it has been bought at the price of blood. Blood that men and women of our country have shed so that the American people can live in the way that they see fit.

ENRICHED INFORMATION THAT OVERFLOWS

Joe's days of being a soldier were indeed numbered, and it was now time that he started giving much deserved attention to his future in the civilian world. This all started with the Army Career and Alumni Program or ACAP for short. The program consisted of three main requirements. The first was to meet with a transitioning guidance counselor and discuss your tentative plans, the second was to attend a five-day intensive workshop, and the third requirement was a two-day job or college workshop. The intent behind the five-day workshop was to provide every service member with the information needed to successfully transition from the military back into the civilian sector. This five-day workshop turned out to be of nominal if not minimal use. Joe was required to sit in a room with 60 to 80 other service members for eight hours per day for five days, without any water or drink, and listen to a person go through slide after slide on a pace that mirrored the speed of Superman. Joe could tell from the very beginning that few of the "instructors" wanted to be there, nor did they fully comprehend the significance of the information they were giving out to the discharging service members. All in all, Joe would estimate that he retained roughly 10 to 15 percent of the priceless information given out in the five-day workshop. The things that he retained consisted mainly of starting a working resume, getting a LinkedIn account, and a brief summary of veterans' benefits that applied specifically to him.

Next came the career or college workshops that every service member was required to attend one or the other. Joe chose to attend the college workshop as he was primarily leaning towards going back to college after the discharge from active duty. This workshop was two days in length and he actually came away with some important information. Joe had applied for the Post 9-11 GI Bill when he was in Afghanistan in the summer of 2013 and had received the Certificate of Eligibility (COE) from the Department of Veteran Affairs. This certificate informed Joe that he was entitled to 90% of the Post 9-11 GI Bill only because he had not completed his third full year of active duty service yet. Upon taking the college workshop (formally known as Furthering Education Workshop) Joe was informed that this 90% eligibility was in fact a mistake and that upon completion of military service he would only be entitled to the Post 9-11 GI Bill at a mere 50%, not 90% rate. This fact was crushing to Joe's future plans as by the time of this college workshop, he had completely invested in the returning to college option for when he transitioned back home to Wisconsin. This class was indeed helpful in identifying the error in Joe's official VA document and saving him countless headaches and hassles in the long run.

KNOWLEDGE IS POWER VIA HELPING HANDS TO A WOUNDED SOLDIER

Joe will never forget one of the instructors of this college workshop, Erin, because she took it upon herself to look further in the state of Wisconsin and after 3 weeks had gone by she emailed him with some amazing news. It seemed Erin had found out that Wisconsin had implemented a State Level Post 9-11 GI Bill which would cover any in-state college tuition that the Federal Post 9-11 GI Bill did not. This meant Joe's plans to return to college were back in and that he would have 50% of his tuition paid for by the Federal and 50% paid for by the WI State GI Bills. At this time, Joe was also in the process of applying for pre-discharge disability benefits and the workshop instructors led me on to a potential Chapter 31- Vocational Rehabilitation. This particular education benefit was given to service members whom had received a service connected disability rating. This benefit is potentially the *most inclusive* of all the educational chapters. The last major benefit that this college workshop had was that during the class every service member was required to apply for educational benefits through the VA's online Website. In addition, the participants had to apply to at least one college or university that they were interested in attending.

STEMMING SUCCESSFUL CAREER WITH STEM EDUCATION AND VOLUNTEERING

Joe was a very meticulous person with choosing which military occupation specialty (MOS) he would learn. Many considerations went into this decision, however, there were a few that stood above the rest. These were, "Am I going to enjoy doing this kind of job for the minimum of the next four years?" "Would I learn a skill that was transferable to the civilian sector?" "Would this skill and experience look good on my resume and therefore make me more marketable?" "Would this MOS fulfill my need for a fulfilling military career?"

After two months of research and countless pieces of advice from his recruiters and other service members, Joe chose the Military Occupational Specialty of 25S, which is STEM-related Satellite Communications Operator Maintainer. This MOS satisfied all of his previously listed considerations. In the meantime, Joe learned that his application to be admitted to the MBA program with IT Management emphasis at the University of Wisconsin was approved. Excited and humbled, Joe felt privileged enough while remembering a priceless piece of information very early in his military career. This information was, "The Army is what you make it SPC Stark, wherever you go and to whichever unit you get assigned, there are many varying perks to each and every duty station... and finally if you want something bad enough you have to go out and take it, do not let anyone tell you NO!" This quote came from Drill Sergeant Cameron Abbott, who was not only the toughest and strictest service member that Joe have ever met, but also the most caring and helpful. Sergeant Abbott's advice led Joe to volunteer for Airborne School and consequently jump out of 17 various aircraft in his army career. This advice also prompted Joe to volunteer, ahead of his companies' rotation, for a deployment to heart of Afghanistan for a Top Secret Mission. This advice stayed with Joe for his entire military career and it continues to affect the way that he thinks today.

MISMATCHED IT AND CYBERSECURITY CERTIFICATIONS

Throughout Joe's service, his unit pushed many "important" cybersecurity and IT certifications onto the soldiers. The individual unit companies' promoted these classes and since the slots were very limited, they made the attendance of these classes very competitive. This competition led to the same select few of the soldiers getting the opportunity to attend said classes and afterward test for the certification. Joe did not appreciate the fact that many of his fellow service members whom were less athletic, intelligent, or personable, got left out of any opportunity to advance their skills as IT and cybersecurity professionals. These classes led to various IT and cybersecurity related certifications include, A +, Network +, Security +, and ICND 1&2 (passing both ICNDs leads to the CISCO certification of CCNA). The Army saw these four certifications as the golden tickets for their service members to transition into highly advanced IT and Cybersecurity professional careers. Joe bought into this logic 100% and it wasn't until sometime later when he met a certain MBA professor at the University of Wisconsin that he realized that this logic, though valuable in the past, may not enable the service members to sufficiently make the cut in today's civilian workplace that is moving rapidly to the virtualized and cloud computing environment.

MUTUAL EDUCATION BETWEEN THE VETERAN AND THE FACULTY

Dr. Ted Lee is Joe's primary professor at the University of Wisconsin's MBA Program for the Information Technology Management emphasis. Dr. Lee and Joe have talked in great depths about the marketable industry certifications that are sought after in the IT arena today. Through the discussions Joe soon came to realize that the four certifications that he had earned through the military were considered more as complements to actually IT and cybersecurity work experience by the industry. The CCNA certification that Joe was especially proud of had become a relatively common entry-level proof of basics of Cisco's proprietary internetwork solution. This went to show that the Army has a rather alarming misconception as to the industry-ready service members which they had previously thought they were producing. Joe enlisted in the Army and therefore he can only speak for the enlisted side of the military. As an enlisted service member, Joe found that the Army actively encourages soldiers to enroll into college and attain their bachelor's degree. This is a fantastic idea, however, out of the 50 plus fellow service members that Joe knew were in school for their bachelor's degree, roughly 45 of them had no clue what college really was. Nearly all of the service members, who enrolled in college, did so under the simple motive of promotion points. The army promotion system is so competitive that those soldiers whom have a bachelor's degree seem to have the advantage in terms of more pay, more responsibility, and consequently better retirement. These soldiers found a college in Texas and another in Maryland which would convert all of their military training into actual college credits for a fee of around $500. So here we have roughly 45 service member who had never attended or enrolled in a single collegiate level class, and they had college transcripts telling the world that they had attained anywhere from 40 to, in some cases, 85 college credit hours. Most of these college credit hours coming from the paid "conversion" of their four IT certifications; A+, Network+,

Security+, and CCNA. All of which, as explained, can guarantee good-paying IT and cybersecurity related jobs in the civilian sector.

A certain sect of people believe that veterans transitioning from active duty back to the civilian sector should be placed in accelerated degree programs. Their justification for the acceleration is the fact that service members come out of the military with an extensive IT background having both job experience as well as industry ready certifications. Joe, along with Ted want to bring attention to the Army, the military, and most importantly all veterans past, present, and future that the accelerated degree programs may not be suitable for all veterans. If one looks on usajobs.com or dice.com and search for any employment under the IT category, it is apparent that less than 10% of the job postings even list the four main Army IT certifications. The percentage is even less if one examines the suggested or required certifications of those same IT job postings.

One thing positive growing out of Joe and Ted's relationship is that not only had Joe learned how to gain advanced knowledge in IT and cybersecurity management that can apply to job functions in civilian workplace, Ted had also learn from Joe what type of training and education Joe has received to perform the daily duties in the Army that Ted wouldn't other get to know. Educating the STEM faculty at the universities on what the veterans went through in the military is a critical step often missing in a successful mentor-mentee relationship.

A ROAD MAP FOR FINDING A PATHWAY TOWARD SUCCESSFUL TRANSITION

There are a number of simple steps that a transitioning service member should follow when his or her contract begins to run out. These steps include:

1) **Apply for Education Benefits through the VA.GOV Website.**
   Whether you are choosing to go straight into the workforce or continuing your education, the most important thing to remember is that the GI-Bill can truly set you up for success at nearly any college, technical school, or university that you choose.

2) **Make contacts ASAP at the schools that you are interested in**. The faculty members and guidance counselors will never know who you are, be able to lend you any advice in terms of your plan or road or to success, or have the opportunity to mentor you unless you contact them and let them know your circumstances. These people will also be able to fill you in immediately about whether that school is Veteran or military friendly. Is that school accommodating of Veterans to include such things as counseling, tutors, guidance, disability accommodations, and even fellow veteran staff members? I have definitely come to realize that no one understands what we have been through while deployed and what we have all experienced in the military, *like a fellow veteran*.

3) **Identify and enable mentorship**. Joe for one was lucky enough to have a caring and mentoring kind of NCO, and that experience led him to reach out to his professors as soon as he arrived at the university. Joe wanted to know what they knew. Joe wanted to learn from them, pick the knowledge from their brains, and in the long run maybe continue educating them something more on what U.S. military experience is about. The value of great mentorship is truly priceless, the benefits are practically countless. When you do eventually decide on a school make sure to find that professor that you can connect and bond with, then ask him or her to be your mentor. The faculty mentor is in the position to provide you with the tools, educational direction, guidance, advice, and even networking with businesses necessary for you to gain that competitive advantage over your peers. Your unit wouldn't deploy you without the best possible equipment or without the most knowledge and training that exists in order for you successfully accomplish the mission. Use this same tactic when choosing the education program, the school, and the pathway that suits you the best.

4) **Work hard toward completing the degree and make the most out of the education**. When Joe graduated college in 2009 with a Bachelor's Degree of Philosophy, he had no clue what he was going to use his degree for or what occupation he could even use it in. Joe joined the military as a satellite communicator and through the Army he attained

the four emphasized certifications. After all was said and done, though Joe was indeed great at the military occupation, through the transition into an MBA program he soon realized that he had a solid but small foundation into the civilian workforce. Joe realized that in order to succeed in the corporate world, he needed to further his education by increasing both IT and cybersecurity core knowledge and business acumen. The MBA program with IT Management emphasis has opened Joe's eyes into what is truly needed in terms of becoming a sought-after IT and cybersecurity professional.

CONCLUSION

Joe and Ted would like to formally make all service members interested in transitioning into IT and cybersecurity in civilian workforce aware of the facts that they have jointly uncovered. There is so much information that Joe would like to share with all his fellow Veterans. Joe feels strongly that, "We have all given years of our lives in service to our country and now it is time that we start our transition back into the civilian world with the right information, the right path way, utilizing all possible tools and benefits available to us, and determining where and how we should start." If Joe had never thought about then actually applied for MBA Program at the University of Wisconsin, je would have never met Dr. Lee. Without Ted's guidance and mentorship Joe would have entered the workforce under-prepared and way behind his peers even with a post-graduate degree at hand.

REFERENCE

[1] Morin, R. (2011). The Difficult Transition from Military to Civilian Life. Retrieved from www.pewsocialtrends.org. - See more at: http://www.ejournalncrp.org/problems-of-combat-veterans-transitioning-to-civilian-life/#sthash.EijDYhHA.dpuf

Partnering for a Seamless Transition to Higher Education: Lessons Learned[1]

Lisa Hoffman, PhD, Associate Professor, UW Tacoma
Mark Brown, EdD candidate, UW Tacoma
Dylan Medina, PhD candidate, UW Seattle

INTRODUCTION

After the Post-9/11 Veterans Educational Benefits were established in 2009, many organizations and higher education institutions asked how such investments could be used most effectively. Such questions were inspired by recognition of the transformational effects of the post–World War II GI Bill benefits that not only supported attendance at colleges and universities, but also refocused attention on access to and the benefits of higher education in America. Recent efforts to improve educational transition include the participants in the NSF project on veteran transition into the engineering and science fields that is the subject of this journal issue.[2] Moreover, as increasing numbers of service members (SM) transitioned out of the military, multi-agency attention focused on how to make this process smoother for the SM and their families. In the state of Washington, the Department of Veterans Affairs (VA) began collaboration with Joint Base Lewis-McChord (JBLM) in 2010 to conduct a review of the transition process for service members in the state. Their review offered several recommendations (see Background section below), including identifying individual plans and tasks in four transition

---

[1] We would like to thank Dylan Medina for his research assistance on this project and his work on an internal report to Joint Base Lewis McChord from the University of Washington Tacoma research team. Lisa Hoffman, PhD was the PI on the program evaluation. Mr. Mark Brown, EdD candidate at UW Tacoma, is focusing his thesis on veteran transition into higher education and career training. He is a civilian employee at JBLM.
[2] See the report Veterans' Education for Engineering and Science: Report of the National Science Foundation Workshop on Enhancing the Post-9/11 Veterans Educational Benefit, April 13, 2009 (http://www.nsf.gov/eng/eec/VeteranEducation.pdf).

tracks: employment, education, career/technical training, and small business/entrepreneurship. In the context of these and other efforts at JBLM, the University of Washington Tacoma (UWT), the largest public university near JBLM, piloted a program of additional career and academic advising for those interested in the higher education track, and conducted an evaluation of this program.[3] The program, UW Tacoma at JBLM Armed Forces Career and Alumni Program (ACAP), consisted of access to a web-based career assessment tool (FOCUS-2), one-on-one career assessment advising, and one-on-one academic guidance for all public two- and four-year colleges and universities in the state of Washington. The program aim was to assist service members, regardless of the higher education institution they planned to attend, in finding the best higher education and career paths for them as individuals.

This paper discusses the findings of the program evaluation, with explicit consideration of wider government and community efforts at improving the transition process. We argue that such concurrently planned efforts underscore the critical importance of community partnerships between colleges, universities, military bases, and their surrounding stakeholders (for-profit and nonprofit) in these efforts. While there is special attention to the impact of partnerships between public higher education and military bases, understanding that these relationships are most effective when they include attention to employment and collaboration with additional partners is essential.

BACKGROUND AND PLANNED CONCURRENT ACTIVITY IN SUPPORT OF THE PROJECT

Since September 11, 2001, the frequency and length of deployments of the U.S. military have increased dramatically. Research indicates that longer and

---

[3] In the spring of 2013, UWT secured Human Subjects Institutional Review Board (IRB) research approval to conduct an evaluation of this program. This paper provides more detailed data from the June 2013-June 2014 formal program evaluation period and summarizes trends and conclusions from the January 2013 to June 2013 program activities, but does not include details about human subjects during this time. The program was first established in November of 2012, but transition services at the base were undergoing curricular and location changes that made the initial implementation of the program slow. We thus begin our summary from January 2013 and include human subject data from June 2013.

more frequent deployments are predictors of greater psychological distress (Childers, 2014). The findings underscore the need for and importance of providing support services for returning veterans, especially those who were deployed to combat zones (Morin, 2011). More than 2.4 million military personnel have been deployed to Iraq, Afghanistan or both theaters. Of that total, more than 1.3 million have since left the military and more than 710,000 have used VA health care between fiscal year 2002 and the third-quarter fiscal year 2011 (Collins et al. 2014).

According to the 2010 Census, just over 2.3 million people, less than one percent of the national population of 308 million, are currently serving in the U.S. military. At the same time, more than 22 million people, seven percent of the national population, are veterans who face a higher rate of unemployment than the national population (Cederhholm, 2013). The unemployment rate of Gulf War-era II veterans of 6.9% exceeded the national average of 5.3% in December 2014

(http://www.bls.gov/news.release/empsit.t05.htm).

The good news is that the rate is down from December 2013, 7.3% for Gulf War-era II veterans compared to 6.4% for nonveterans. The state of Washington, however, ranks in the top four states in the US for Army unemployment costs, highlighting the importance of collaborative attention to the transition process. At present, approximately 8,000 service members transition from active duty each year from Joint Base Lewis-McChord (JBLM) in Washington State, a figure that is expected to continue through 2017.[4]

---

[4] To help address these issues, Governor Inslee signed his first Executive order in office at JBLM on May 10th, 2013, Executive Order 13-01, Veterans, and State Employment http://www.governor.wa.gov/office/execorders/), to help tackle transition issues. It requires each executive cabinet agency to develop a veteran employment plan to increase the representation of veterans in their workforce. Each agency must report progress as prescribed by the Office of the State Human Resources Director (OSHRD.) It augments a review of job applicants' qualifications to consider relevant equivalent experience obtained during military service. OSHRD assists staff and hiring managers to translate and credit military experience. OSHRD must collaborate with the Departments of Enterprise Services (DES), Employment Security (ESD), and Veterans Affairs (DVA), as well as other public and private partners to identify and develop veterans employment strategies and resources. It also established the Washington State Military Transition Council (WSMTC)

These military personnel represent a diverse racial and ethnic population, with 36% minority male and female composition.[5]

There are several critical moments to note in governance of the transition process. In June 2010, JBLM asked the Washington State Department of Veteran Affairs (WDVA) to conduct a Lean Six Sigma (LSS) process improvement review of the military transition process. The results of this review were a comprehensive improvement plan and recommended process change.[6] The key components of the recommendations were:

- service members must start the process earlier (at least 12 months prior to separation);

- better preparation to enter civilian sector;

- networking;

- Individual Transition Plan (ITP) development (realistic options);

- service member empowerment, awareness and risk mitigation;

- timely decision-making (including reenlistment opportunities);

- replacement or elimination of long, static briefings with experiential, kinetic, one-on-one customer service that resonates with a 20-30 year old service member;

- reduce effects of service member unemployment claims (UCX) that impact DOD's budget;

- and increase command support.

Immediately following the JBLM review, the Vice Chief of Staff Army (VCSA) General Peter Chiarelli directed the Army G-1 to conduct a total review of the Army's transition process. A United States Military Academy (USMA) study group concurred with the JBLM improvement plan,

---

(http://www.dva.wa.gov/about-wdva/washington-state-military-transition-council-wsmtc) which meets quarterly to coordinate transition assistance programs between Washington's military bases and other key stakeholders.

[5] Based on internal government data.

[6] This transition chart is available at http://www-stage.dva.wa.gov/sites/default/files/WA%20State%20ACAP%20Transition%20Map%20-%20JUNE%202014.jpg.

identifying it as an Army best practice, and recommending Army-wide implementation. Concurrently, JBLM worked with Washington State Senator Murray's staff to highlight the shortcomings of ACAP, a system that had not been reviewed since its inception in 1992, when it was created to address military transition challenges for the post-Cold War/Gulf War-era. The creation of ACAP was a significant improvement over the existing Army Continuing Education System (ACES), created in 1973 to address the transition challenges post-Vietnam (Anderson & Kime, 1996).

The Veteran Opportunity to Work to Hire Heroes Act of 2011 (VOW Act) was then passed as Public Law 112-56 (VOW To Hire Heroes Act 2011).[7] The VOW Act directed improvement of the DOD's Transition Assistance Program (TAP). It also made completion of TAP *mandatory* for transitioning service members, upgraded career counseling options and resume writing skills, and ensured that the program was tailored for the 21st century job market (Hodne, Lieutenant Colonel Daniel C, 2013). The VOW Act aimed to facilitate a seamless transition so that service members can begin the process prior to separation at jobs with VA, Homeland Security, and many other federal agencies. It expanded education and training, and provided additional benefits for unemployed and disabled veterans.[8] The VOW Act required the Department of Labor (DOL) to make military skills and training translatable into the civilian sector and simplify the process to obtain licenses and certifications. It also provided tax credits of up to $5,600 for hiring veterans, and up to $9,600 for hiring disabled veterans, if the veteran had been looking for work for six months or longer. These incentives are important as they have adjusted the landscape of transition for service members. It is in this context that the UWT pilot project was conceived and implemented.

---

[7] This bill combined provisions of Senator Murray's Hiring Heroes Act (S. 951; Report #112-36), and Chairman Miller's Veterans Opportunity to Work Act (H.R. 2433; Report #112-242), and veterans' tax credits into a single package that targeted the high rate of veteran's unemployment (Weaver, 2013).

[8] For instance, unemployed veterans of past war eras were provided with up to one year of additional Montgomery GI Bill benefits to qualify for jobs in high-demand sectors. It also provided disabled veterans up to one year of additional vocational rehabilitation and employment benefits.

Additionally, in December 2011, JBLM participated in the Army Transition Summit hosted by the VCSA, General Chiarelli at the Pentagon. The focused outcomes of the summit were: creation and implementation of a Department of the Army Execution Order (DA EXORD) for transition policy; evaluation and selection of a single portal technology application; revision of the TAP workshop; and identification of resource gaps to implement improved processes. In that same month, the DA EXORD was released with revised and expanded policy for transition services. The revision was based closely on the initial recommendations of the JBLM process improvement plan and the USMA study group, recognizing the innovations and partnerships put into place at this installation. The key components of revision included:

- initiation of transition process earlier (at least 12 months prior to separation instead of the previous requirement of 90 days);

- emphasis on command involvement and support;

- institution of measures of effectiveness tracked in the ACAP XXI software system;

- mandatory benefits enrollment for VA and DOL services;

- initial counseling (ACAP) and development of the Individual Transition Plan (ITP);

- attendance at the VA Benefits Briefing and a resume for 100% of transitioning soldiers;

- and requirement for soldiers to register for eBENEFITS at (https://www.ebenefits.va.gov) and myHEALTHeVET at (www.myhealth.va.gov).

With the passage of The VOW Act in November 2011, and the subsequent passing of Public Law 112-56, the DOD and DHS gained authority to permit participation in apprenticeship programs for transitioning service members. We include a description of a successful apprenticeship program initiated at JBLM as an example of effective partnering for transition services. JBLM requested and received Staff Judge Advocate legal clearance to conduct apprenticeship programs. LTG Bromberg, Army G1, approved JBLM as a VIP pilot site. The Secretary of the Army convened an Apprenticeship Task Force to outline the path forward. The United Association of Journeymen and Apprentices of the Plumbing and Pipe Fitting Industry of the United States, Canada and Australia (UA) (http://uavip.org/) piloted the concept at Camp Pendleton, California, Camp Murray, and JBLM to create the UA VIP Program that provides 18 weeks of accelerated welding and Heating, Ventilation, Air Conditioning and Refrigeration (HVAC/R) career and technical training. The training is free to transitioning service members who are placed in careers nationwide, replacing an aging workforce. Well-trained and highly-skilled welders and HVAC/R technicians are in high demand nationwide. The first JBLM accelerated welding class began in January 2013 at the UA Local 26 Training Facility in Lacey, Washington. Follow-on classes are every 20 weeks. Fort Carson, Colorado started the VIP program and a welding class commenced in October 2013. The UA expanded the VIP program to Fort Hood, Texas in February 2014. Fort Campbell, Kentucky is the next location for national expansion. The UA's welding and HVAC/R apprenticeship programs are certified for college credit with Washtenaw Community College, Ann Arbor, Michigan. Ongoing college credit is earned by the apprentice throughout their career and fully funded by the UA. Students attending the VIP program train for 18 weeks in order to earn six semester hours of college credit toward an Associate's degree, enter the UA's five-year apprenticeship program upon successful completion, and work in journey-level apprenticeship jobs, earning a living wage of salary and benefits. Entry-level apprentices can earn up to half of the living wage of journeypersons in their skilled trade for the geographic area. Following the completion of each year as a successful apprentice, salaries increase approximately 10% until journey-level wages are reached at the completion of the apprenticeship. The UA's apprenticeship appointments are eligible for GI Bill payment from the VA. The program received national recognition recently on NBC Nightly News

(http://www.millerwelds.com/resources/articles/UA-Veterans-in-Piping-Program-VIP-Trains-Veterans/).

JBLM started the Microsoft Software & Systems Academy (MSSA) in 2013, which consists of a 16-week course to obtain the certification required for technology careers such as a developer, applications engineer and IT project manager. Saint Martin's University delivers the content at JBLM during the duty day. The program will expand to other bases in the nation, starting with California and Texas. Active duty, National Guard and Reserves from all branches of the military are eligible for the academy

(http://www.microsoft.com/en-us/news/press/2013/nov13/11-04softwaresystemsacademypr.aspx).

OVERVIEW OF THE PROJECT

The pilot program offered by UWT at JBLM's ACAP must be understood in the context of these federal and DOD initiatives. In addition, it may be helpful to think of the services offered in terms of how a college student experiences "extra electives." The "required" coursework – coming out of the VOW Act requirements – consisted of more than five days of transition classes, including an intake process, an orientation session, classes from the Department of Labor, classes from the VA, and classes organized by their chosen track (Higher Education, Career/Technical Training, Small Business / Entrepreneurship, and Standard Employment). Thus, any additional meetings with UWTstaff were above an already demanding transition services schedule. Moreover, these UWT services and the surveys related to the program evaluation were all done on a voluntary basis. Both of these factors limited the number of service members who participated.

Conducting this program evaluation alerted us to additional valuable outcomes. In particular, we believe that there is significant value to having a higher education specialist in proximity to the TAP counselors, who are primarily DOD contract workers and often not long-term employees. This value is both because UWT placed a seasoned specialist in in the transition services center with deep and detailed knowledge of military transition/benefits and higher education in Washington, and because the service member sees evidence of partnership between his/her base and the higher education civilian community. Please see further discussion of key findings and recommendations below.

In this pilot program, UWT advisers made contact with transitioning service members in group sessions, through drop-ins, and in one-on-one appointments at ACAP. From January to June 2013, a general "career log" to assess plans was used, and then the service member was offered access to UWT's FOCUS-2 web-based career assessment tool, as well as one-on-one follow up sessions to discuss the results. FOCUS-2 produces a personality and career profile of users and attempts to match them to potential career and education paths. For the academic services, the UWT staff used a general "higher education log" to assess the service member's knowledge about higher education and funding resources. The service member was then offered general and one-to-one advising and discussions of educational pathways at all public 2- and 4-year institutions in the state. Information about how to fund their education was also provided in group and individual sessions.

ENGAGING EXTRA SERVICES

If service members chose to participate in the pilot program (whether they were study participants or not), they were asked routine questions about their career and higher education plans and goals. A number of participants also opted to start the FOCUS-2 assessment tool, but most did not complete it. Starting in June 2013, we began the formal program evaluation by recruiting voluntary study participants to take additional intake and exit surveys. Participants were divided into two subject groups – the advising group and the comparison group. The advising group refers to all study participants who met with UWT staff at ACAP and received career assessment advising and/or advising on any public higher education institution in the state of Washington. These study participants should have completed an intake survey and an exit survey upon completion of their interactions with UWT staff or their separation from the military. The comparison group refers to those who did NOT meet with any UWT staff and did not use any of the UWT services in ACAP. They completed one exit survey as they turned in their final paperwork and out-processed. Participation in both groups was entirely voluntary.

This report also includes summary information about the more informal and drop-in advising done consistently by the UWT staff. It is this more informal advising that seems to be the most beneficial and timely, as it takes place during the service member's initial orientation with their ACAP counselor.

PROGRAM EVALUATION ADVISING GROUP

Forty-four people who met with UWT staff for services voluntarily became study participants, this is the advising group. All 44 study participants signed consent forms and completed intake surveys, but only 11 completed exit surveys. In the fall of 2014 we conducted follow-up outreach to secure exit surveys from those who had signed consent forms and indicated a willingness to be contacted. Only two individuals returned the exit surveys, increasing this to a total of 13. Another 11 surveys were returned, but they either did not sign consent forms or did not complete them properly. The data from those surveys are not included here. Overall these are very disappointing study numbers, which we believe is due to several factors outlined in this report (e.g., participation is voluntary).

General demographics for this group include: 82% male; average age of 37; 86% had at least one deployment; 54% were leaving because of retirement and 26% were transitioning because of ETS; 74% were currently married and 17% had never married; and just 14% had only a high school diploma or GED.

PROGRAM EVALUATION COMPARISON GROUP

Thirty-eight people who never took advantage of UWT services in ACAP voluntarily completed our comparison group exit survey. They received a copy of the consent form with project information and are considered study participants. These surveys show an overall positive response to the information and guidance received in the ACAP transition process. For instance, in responding to the statement "before the ACAP transition process, I felt unclear about my career path after leaving the military," 10 reported "neutral," 6 reported "agree," and 4 "reported strongly agree." Yet in answering questions about feeling more prepared and aware after the transition process, the answers were strongly in favor of agreement. For example 12 reported "strongly agree" and 10 reported "agree" in regards to the statement "I have now identified skills from my military experience that can be applied to my career(s) of interest"; and 13 reported "strongly agree" and 8 reported "agree" in regards to the statement "I have now identified personal career goals."

General demographics for this group include: 84% male and 16% female; average age was 29; 82% had at least one deployment; 55% were transitioning because of ETS; 58% were currently married and 24% had never married; and 10 individuals who reported having completed an ACAP track noted they started in a different track.

THE VALUE OF INFORMAL COUNSELING AND A "WARM HAND-OVER"

The above numbers demonstrate that service members are not interested in taking surveys or completing career assessment tools that may be detailed and time-consuming unless they are required. Finally, there is a general reluctance to add another scheduled class or appointment to a transition process that already demands over five days of their time. Nevertheless, the UWT advisory staff member noted that after having established a level of trust with the ACAP counselors, they would bring service members directly to her with higher education questions. The counselors would also stop in to talk with her about higher education. It is critical to note that this staff person was deliberately and well-trained to provide information about all public higher education institutions in the state while in this role. This program took this generalized and unbiased advising role very seriously. Because predatory practices by some educational entities and competition between higher education institutions serving veterans and military can be detrimental to the implementation of programs aimed at transition, this should be addressed in each community.

In order to try to quantify what seemed like a significant contribution to the transition process, the staff member recorded what she referred to as "drop-in" meetings with service members when she was able to provide significant information to them. For instance, in October and November 2013, 44 individuals met with the staff person in "drop-in" appointments; and in February, March, and April 2014, 54 drop-in appointments were recorded. The total for this time period (October 2013 to mid-July 2014) was 147 recorded meetings.

Additionally, the research team created a list of veteran center contacts at *all* public 2- and 4- year institutions of higher education in the state of Washington. The program staff used this regularly to provide what is termed a "warm hand-over" for the service member. Specifically, she gave the service member the name and contact information of individuals in the veteran service center and/or admissions office at the school. Research indicates that this kind of information and a "warm hand-over" and "mentor-based" process is especially effective for the veteran and military population.[9] It has been operationalized by the VA in states such as Minnesota as well

(see: http://www.mnveteranservice.org/documents/
Veterans_Coordinators.html).

Moreover, this kind of experience in the transition process helps to place the service member in a wider "community of care." One study suggests practices of *listening* to the service members' stories and experiences, and bringing in all relevant campus services (termed "everybody plays") can be very effective in successful transition (Moon and Schma 2011).

SUMMARY OF KEY FINDINGS AND BUILDING A "MODEL OF PARTNERSHIP"

While sample sizes are limited in all sections of this report, we argue here that patterns emerge that provide insights into the UWT program specifically, and may be generalizable to military transition more broadly. Moreover, we suggest there are key elements of this program that may provide a model of how large public universities should be partnering with regional military bases.

---

[9] See Burnett and Segoria 2009; Anderson 2012; Green and Hayden 2013; Moon and Schma 2011.

Key findings include:

- **Most service members reported having no prior career or education guidance.**[10] This guidance is crucial to facilitate transition because it helps service members become more aware of the potential paths they might take upon transitioning out of the service. <u>This suggests that increased and earlier guidance</u> could make the transition less abrupt.

- **Most service members indicated interest in educational pathways.** Research shows that in general a majority of service members entered the military, at least in part, for the education benefits (Taylor 2011). JBLM statistics indicate that upon transition, approximately 40% of service members enroll in full time education, and an additional 13% enroll in part time education while working a full or part time job. However, there is some question as to what education options they are aware of and what their goal is in pursuing higher education. It is clear that many of them see higher education as a key to upward mobility. <u>Offering proximate specialization in higher education during transition, as well as earlier higher education advising and enrollment opportunities, would be useful for service members</u>.

- **Service members clearly gravitated toward group advising settings rather than one-on-one sessions.** An overemphasis on group classes was present both in the early phases of the UWT program and in ACAP more generally, with advising staff transitioning to more one-on-one appointments starting in the fall of 2013. <u>More one-on-one and "buddy" advising and mentoring could be useful</u>.

- Group classes are useful sites for collaboration, providing general information and a less intimidating environment. However, they often ignore the unique situation of each individual.

- One-on-one sessions are useful because they provide tailored information unique to the needs of the individual. Moreover, research has demonstrated that service members' transitions happen more smoothly with one-on-one advising and mentoring (Johnson 2009; DiRamio, Ackerman and Mitchell 2008).

---

[10] This comes primarily from summaries by the program staff over the duration of the program, rather than the intake and exit surveys done by study participants.

- A "buddy" system of 2 or 3 service members making appointments to discuss individual interests together may also be an effective form of advising and mentoring.

- **There is a sense that ACAP and the UWT Program operate in ways that may privilege particular paths and fields.** A general emphasis on "higher demand industries" and STEM fields may limit the options that service members would wish to consider. Tools such as FOCUS-2 could help service members. <u>More individual or "buddy" advising, coupled with a mandatory career assessment tool, may be effective</u>.

- **A "warm hand-over" from the transition process to higher education institutions may ease the transition for service members.** This requires keeping an updated list of individuals and contact information for the veteran and military service centers at all public higher education institutions in the state. Other innovative programs at JBLM, such as apprenticeship programs, offer a similar hand-over directly into the civilian working world.[11] Similar to experiences of civilian first-generation college students, many service members are unfamiliar with higher education processes, terminology and culture (Anderson 2012). <u>Continuing with this direct contact through the transition process should be useful</u>.

PART ONE: CAREER ASSESSMENT ADVISING

Discussion of Findings and Recommendations:

A finding of this study is that service members are getting career assessment and advising only at the end of their service period. While a little bit of advising late is better than none at all, having advising *at the end of service* places a greater emphasis on *the break* than on the transition to the next phase, creating a feeling that the *distance* of the transition is extended. Additionally, service members facing transition likely have limited attention and time they can put toward the career assessments and advising.

---

[11] See the following link for praise for this apprenticeship program:
http://www.dvidshub.net/news/137474/sma-chandler-blown-away-armys-job-placement-pilot-program#.U9Z64eNdV8.

More frequent and earlier career advising could help service members begin to think about what kinds of skills and experiences they gain in the military and how those skills might be re-contextualized to civilian settings. Paying attention to transition earlier will make it more gradual, allowing service members to feel that they can bring more of what they learned in the military with them.

The process of encountering a situation – such as separation from the military – that requires action and determination of effective strategies to respond is referred to as "uptake" in academic literature (Freadman 2002). Individuals assess the situation and select a response, based on memories of past similar experiences. If past transitions have had a positive impact on the individual, then they will "take up" this transition to civilian life in a more positive manner; the opposite may also be true. An individual may be unable to connect the present situation to anything in their memory, and thus, if they "take up" this unknown negatively, they may select strategies of avoidance and resistance. A Pew survey (Morin, 2011) in 2011 found that 44% of veterans who served since 9/11 had trouble adjusting to civilian life, underscoring the difficulty of this process (Collins et al. 2014).

This notion is also important because transition itself means movement from one context or social reality to another. Service member's memories - or knowledge of the rules - must be sufficiently generalized to be used to connect or explain the demands of the new context, otherwise he or she will struggle to select effective actions in the new context. In addition, the last major transition the service member experienced when he or she joined the military was a highly structured one. This is distinctly different from what is expected in the transition to civilian life, which emphasizes individuality and unique pathways. Providing a longer transition process may help create less of a break and more of a *transition*.

Academic writings about transitions from one social status to another also describe the transition itself as having a "liminal" period (Turner 1987). Liminality refers to a state of "in-between-ness" when one is moving from one status or identity (e.g., child) to another (e.g., adult). Rituals and rites of passage, such as graduation ceremonies, can be particularly important in marking the end of the liminal, or in-between, phase and celebrating the new identity. ACAP thus may be understood as a liminal phase of "in-between-ness" or transition from a military-dominant identity to a more civilian-dominant identity. Recognizing the refiguring of the self that takes place in this process and marking the completion of this transition with "graduation" events may be helpful for the service members.

No previous career advising

Career guidance is important, particularly for a transition that may be problematic for service members. Guidance is particularly crucial because it can help service members learn what is possible in civilian spaces and what kinds of pathways are available to them. However, a majority (76%) of those asked had never received career advising prior to this program. Similar proportions had never taken a career assessment (77%) or been to a career fair (72%). Of those who had received prior career exploration services, females were slightly less likely to have taken a career assessment or been to a career fair.

The proportion of individuals who had never received previous career exploration services suggests that little attention is paid to transitioning into a civilian career until the end of an individual's term of service. Since concern for transition only becomes formalized when service members enter ACAP, there is a distinct divide between military and civilian experience. This sharp division may make the transition more distant, and may make it more difficult for service members to think about how their military experiences and skills can be modified and applied to civilian life.

Dominance of group advising

A significant majority of service members who met with UWT advisors did so in group rather than individual sessions. This has much to do with the structure of the program that required service members to hear their presentations at the end of a regular session. Moreover, individual appointments required both additional personal time and attendance without peer support. While additional one-on-one advising sessions were not popular in general, it was even rarer for individuals to attend an individual session after attending a group session.

Yet, studies suggest that service members' transitions (e.g., into higher education settings) are best facilitated by one-on-one interaction with each individual (see Ackerman and DiRamio 2009). While group sessions are valuable against an alternative of little or no guidance, they do not adequately address individual needs and interests. It is possible that group settings include peer pressure to push people into a limited range of fields.

A "buddy" system of 2 to 3 service members attending individualized advising together may help provide tailored information and access the advantages noted in such an approach to transition. Individualized advice and guidance is clearly crucial for service members who likely only have a limited sense of what they are capable of doing in the civilian world. This is particularly true if they enlisted out of high school or college. Having easy access to individualized advising, guidance, and mentoring is crucial to helping service members figure out how they will take what they have learned in the military and apply it to their path in the civilian sphere. Moreover, peer pressure associated with a group might push individuals into popular career paths that do not really interest them.

FOCUS-2 web-based career assessment tool

The FOCUS-2 tool is a web-based personal, career, and education assessment tool. This tool consists of 14 sections with questionnaires that request users respond with a degree of interest in particular topics or activities. The tool provides personality, career, and education profiles that "fit" the individual. The second half of the program, which produces the career and educational profile, also generates a list of options for the user to browse. Completing all sections takes a good deal of time, particularly if the user is reading carefully and considering the options provided. Access to this tool was provided free of charge to JBLM service members going through ACAP as a part of this UWT program.

While this tool cannot approximate the responsiveness of quality one-on-one advising, it can produce a useful profile, particularly when coupled with individualized advising. The profile thus can be used to help direct the advising. The tool covers a broad range of topics and includes questions about one's leisure interests as well. It also provides average salaries of careers and the rate of growth in a field. It does, however, privilege certain fields that are considered "high demand," such as STEM fields.

FOCUS-2 participation and recommendations

A total of 114 individuals from JBLM created FOCUS-2 accounts, with 90 created in 2013 and 24 created in 2014 through July 20. Only three people completed all sections of the questionnaire; 99 people started the questionnaire; 43 completed half (7) or more of the sections; and 15 individuals registered, but completed no sections. In the program evaluation study exit surveys, six individuals claimed to have completed the program (compared to administrative access to FOCUS-2 that confirmed only three people had completed all sections). Of those six, three said it was helpful. Those who found it useful were either neutral or unclear about their path after separating from the military. Those who did not find it helpful were the least positive in terms of self-knowledge and two of them trended towards disagree and strongly disagree on the exit survey set questions. The negative responses may be related more to a general negative attitude about the transition process, rather than to a specific transition service. To assess if there are generalizable benefits from this tool, we suggest it be made mandatory. Mandatory completion of the tool would provide all service members going through ACAP with a detailed profile and extensive list of potential career and education paths that likely match fairly well their personal interests. It is clear that FOCUS-2 does not attract enough interest on its own. It is also clear that many individuals do not complete the assessment without encouragement. Making the tool mandatory is likely the most effective way to get service members to take advantage of such a resource.

PART TWO: HIGHER EDUCATION ADVISING

Discussion of Findings and Recommendations:

Based on this program evaluation and discussions with the advisors, this report concludes that there is strong interest in higher education among transitioning service members. JBLM statistics also indicate that upon transition, approximately 40% of service members enroll in full time education and an additional 13% enroll in part time education while working a full or part time job. For instance, based on data from the "logs," 72% were considering either 4 year or graduate degrees, with an additional 23% considering 2 year degrees (both transferable and terminal). Of those interested in graduate work, approximately one quarter were interested in medicine and law. Additionally, 89% planned on using the Post-9/11 GI Bill benefits; and of those who answered the questions, 63% knew about the higher education system in Washington; 26% said they did not know the difference between public and private for-profit institutions; and 32% did not know about the 2+2 transfer system in the state. This interest in higher education matches the 75% of post-9/11 veterans who claim that education benefits were a major reason for joining the military (Taylor 2011). Moreover, after the Post-9/11 Bill Benefits were established, schools have predicted and seen rapidly increasing numbers of veterans and dependents enrolling in higher education.

In general, service members responded positively about the importance of higher education as a part of their pathway, and according to advising group exit survey, those considering further education felt well informed about admissions and financial aid procedures. This may reflect information gathered in the new higher education track classes as well.

Higher education and transition

While the majority of those meeting with the program advisor had at least some college experience, the majority of it was from community and military colleges. Moreover, approximately half were choosing a field that was different from their military specialty. This is noteworthy and also suggests the importance of individualized, one-on-one advising rather than group advising sessions that may promote group think and peer pressure. To some extent, this could reflect a desire to try something new, which is a disposition useful for transitioning effectively because it allows individuals to try out the customs of new social contexts in the civilian sphere. While the exit survey data from the program evaluation study indicates service members feel they have learned valuable skills during their military careers, it is not entirely clear which skills they find most useful. When connected to the study released by the PEW Research Center (2011), this further emphasized the sense that service members overwhelmingly value their military experience but struggle to see exactly how that experience applies directly to future professions with the exception of skills such as work ethic and teamwork.

This evaluation also suggests that service members need to be well versed in the differences between higher education institutions so that they are able to make the transition from base-oriented schools to additional educational options in their communities. Considering the notion of "uptake," service members with the tools to see similarities between their past and future higher education experiences should experience more successful transitions. They will, however, need to understand the differences between community colleges, military colleges, baccalaureate institutions, and graduate schools. In addition, earlier emphasis on higher education, coupled with greater opportunities for enrollment, may decrease the feeling of "distance" in the transition to traditional colleges and universities.

Summary and Recommendations

This study is a part of a longer tradition of studies of the military that help us to understand social changes in America. For instance, past studies have documented the impact of the post-WWII GI Bill benefits; shifting social mores with public attitudes towards the military during and after the Vietnam War; and questions of social mobility, especially for minorities, with the All-Volunteer Force (AVF) after the Vietnam War (M. A. Kleykamp, 2006).[12] Yet

---

[12] Some argue this is true because military service offers both steady employment and numerous benefits such as the GI Bill (Kleykamp 2009). For example, Air Force training for enlisted personnel to prepare them for their technical specialties can be applied toward an

research on the military has been surprisingly limited since Vietnam, particularly in the past decade, except for a focus on Post Traumatic Stress Disorder and Traumatic Brain Injury. The military remains a major institution in the lives of many young people, with roughly 200,000 new recruits entering the ranks each year (M. A. Kleykamp, 2006).

The academic advising provided by the UWT program at ACAP sought to orient service members to these issues and to find the best education pathway for them as individuals. Being able to navigate the various options available for higher education is a crucial part of transition. For instance, even though there is a strong interest in further education, few had taken the steps necessary to get their paperwork, such as past transcripts, in order. Although a significant number that had not yet requested them knew how to do so, most desired an unofficial review of their transcripts to help them understand what might be transferable to a BA. Additionally, similar to the career assessment advising experience, few had robust advising histories. This suggests that earlier and holistic higher education advising for service members that includes information both about how to earn degrees while on active duty and how those options may change after transition (e.g., a focus on brick and mortar institutions in their communities) would be useful.

Partnership between a military installation and a higher education institution can support such advising. With significant interest in and financial support for higher education, robust guidance to service members is absolutely vital. In the dominant culture it is natural to see higher education as the path to career success, but this perspective is also challenged by mixed data on veteran success rates and student loan concerns. Finally, the "warm hand-over" that advisors in this program were able to provide to admissions and veteran center staff at all 2 and 4 year public institutions in the state is a valuable asset in this process. We suggest other states create up-to-date contact lists.

While data are limited in this study, several general conclusions may be drawn. It is clear that it is difficult to get service members to take advantage of

---

associate's degree through the Community College of the Air Force, which is an accredited degree-granting institution

additional advising and other services. There are likely a number of factors at work, including a lack of history with advising, an emphasis on this transition as a rupture or break rather than a transition, and limited ability to relate past experiences to the new civilian context.

Regarding "uptake," understanding one's situation and the rules in new settings requires a degree of self-knowledge and confidence, which may be enhanced with earlier and more robust career and academic advising. If memories suggest that moving into a new space will be interesting, challenging, and enjoyable, it is more likely the service member will be successful.

Movement from one context to a new context also clearly requires redefining one's self and having a strong sense of how past skills and knowledge may be used and modified in the new setting. The general consensus is that no matter how we see transitions working, being aware of what is going on is a crucial component to transitioning successfully (Beach 2003; Devitt 2007; Nowacek 2011; Tuomi-Grohn and Engestrom 2003). We also suggested the concept of liminality as a way to think about the process of transition. Liminality refers to an in-between or liminal state as someone moves from one status or identity (e.g., military) to another (e.g., civilian), which often includes specific rites of passage. In using this concept, we suggested, for instance, providing group-based rites of passage that reference the camaraderie produced when one joins the military combined with one-on-one advising that addresses the specific concerns of each individual. Providing this continuous support as individuals gradually move through this liminal space between military and civilian settings could help develop smoother transition experiences. Earlier emphasis on how military experience (specific to specialty and generalized in terms of teamwork and leadership) can be modified or re-contextualized for civilian settings should also help with this process, emphasizing transition rather than rupture. Celebrating the transition formally may also help solidify the new civilian-oriented status.

Finally, we conclude that not much concern has been paid to transition prior to service members encounter with ACAP. Respondents in this report generally have some familiarity with the transition process including financial aid options, education options, and career options. Additionally, they are generally aware of what paperwork needs to be completed (e.g., collecting transcripts), but also generally have not completed such work. Concomitantly, many have not experienced career or academic assessment in the past. This suggests that service members are aware that the transition is coming, but have not done much to work on it by the time they reach ACAP.

If thought of transition occurs only at the very edge of each experience, it will appear more drastic when it is taken up. Much of the avoidance and lack of enthusiasm present in the data suggests that such a situation exists. Without question, new programs and classes put into place by ACAP in the past year have improved this greatly.

Building Partnerships

Working across the fence of the military installation as partners to address issues related to veteran transition is essential for veterans' success. We believe this project and the recommendations listed below can be a model for other regions. Other key initiatives implemented by JBLM and UWT to support the transition process of service members include a job shadow program named Northwest Edge developed in partnership with Dylan Medina, from the University of Washington Seattle, and Hire America's Heroes (http://hireamericasheroes.org/). JBLM also works with several local private sector companies to expand our mentorship programs in cooperation with Boots to Shoes (http://www.bootstoshoes.org/). This regional community networking forum provides opportunities to connect veterans, transitioning service members, regional education institutions, and local Chambers of Commerce, Veteran Service Organizations, and community businesses. JBLM and UWT also work with local non-profits like Tacoma's Rally Point 6 (http://rp6communitysitrep.blogspot.com/) and grant-funded organizations like Camo to Commerce (http://www.pacmtn.org/camo-2-commerce/) to help transitioning service members.

Recommendations from this program evaluation:

- **Address the transition earlier and with greater resources**; service members will have the opportunity to begin to develop a higher level of awareness of their own experiences as well as the potential challenges of the transition.

- **Require career assessment and educational advising earlier**; service members may be unclear about the value of these activities. Earlier exposure will help familiarize them with these services and make separation less of a rupture and more of a transition.

- **Shift more emphasis to one-on-one and "buddy" advising, along with some group sessions**; while this requires more resources, a buddy system may make it easier for some service members to attend additional sessions.

- **Work to address the ideological forces that limit potential paths into civilian life**; service members will have a variety of interests ranging from STEM fields to the Humanities to Business. All of these should be treated as viable options. Service members should feel free to explore fields that are outside of their military specialty.

- **Make a career assessment tool mandatory**; FOCUS-2 or other personality, career, and education assessment tool should be used completely.

- **Continue to establish partnerships among civilian, academic, and military institutions because they can do much to facilitate transition**; community partners will provide familiar channels through which service members can make their transitions. Partnerships will also make it easier for service members to gain a sense of how they will need to adapt. Non-military institutions learn to be more flexible and accepting of the efforts service members make. A good example is the scheduling of visits to schools and other relevant institutions by the higher education and career and technical tracks.

The views expressed in this article are those of the authors and do not reflect the official policy or position of the Department of the Army, DOD, or the U.S. Government.

REFERENCES

[1] Anderson, J. (2012). Warriors in the Academy: Veterans Transition from the Military to Higher Education. Master of Arts Thesis, Sociology, George Mason University.

[2] Ackerman, R. and DiRamio, D. (2009) *Creating a Veteran-Friendly Campus: Strategies for Transition and Success. New Directions for Student Services*, 126. San Francisco: Jossey-Bass

[3] Anderson, C. L., & Kime, S. F. (1996). "Some major contributions of the military to the field of adult and continuing education in the United States (A work in progress)" *Conference Proceedings*, Annual Meeting of the American Association for Adult and Continuing Education, Oct 31, 1996 (http://www.editlib.org/p/82498/).

[4] Beach, K. (2003) "Consequential Transitions: Developing a View of Knowledge Propagation through Social Organizations." In T. Tuomi-Grohn and Y. Engestrom. (Eds.), *Between Work and School: New Perspectives on Transfer and Boundary-Crossing.* (39-61). San Francisco: Pergamon.

[5] Bowling, U. B., & Sherman, M. D. (2008). Welcoming them home: Supporting service members and their families in navigating the tasks of reintegration. *Professional Psychology: Research and Practice*, 39(4), 451.

[6] Burnett, S. E., & Segoria, J. (2009). Collaboration for Military Transition Students from Combat to College: It Takes a Community. *Journal of Postsecondary Education and Disability*, 22(1), 53-58.

[7] Childers, A. K. (2013). *Effects of Deployment on Student Veterans' Levels of Perceived Stress, Coping Styles, Sense of Coherence, and Perceived Quality of Life*, Middle Tennessee State University, MA Thesis.

[8] Collins, Benjamin, and Robert Jay Dilger, Cassandria Dortch, Lawrence Kapp, Sean Lowry (2014) "Employment for Veterans: Trends and Programs," *Cornell University ILR School Digital Commons@ILR*, http://digitalcommons.ilr.cornell.edu/cgi/viewcontent.cgi?article=2245&context=key_workplace (Accessed April 20, 2015).

[9] Davis, R. N. (2013). Veterans fighting wars at home and abroad. *Texas Tech Law Review* 45(2).

[10] Devitt, A. (2007) "Transferability and Genres." In C. J. Keller and C. R. Weisser (Eds). *The Locations of Composition.* (215-28) New York: SUNY Press.

[11] DiRamio, D., R. Ackerman, & R. L. Mitchell. (2008). From Combat to Campus: Voices of Student-Veterans. *NASPA Journal*, 45(1), 73-102.

[12] Freadman 2002, "Uptake," in R.M. Coe, L. Lingard, and T. Teslenko (Eds.), *The Rhetoric and Ideology of Genre*, Cresskill: Hampton, pp. 39-53.

[13] Green, L. E. I. G. H., & Hayden, S. E. T. H. (2013). Supporting student veterans: Current landscape and future directions. *Journal of Military and Government Counseling*, 1(2), 89.

[14] Heaton, P., & Krull, H. (2012). "Unemployment among Post-9/11 Veterans and Military Spouses after the Economic Downturn," *RAND National Defense Research Institute*, Occasional Paper, 1-12 (http://www.rand.org/content/dam/rand/pubs/occasional_papers/2012/RAND_OP376.pdf).

[15] Hodne, Lieutenant Colonel Daniel C. (2013). *We want you: It takes a village to market the army* Strategy Research Project, US Army War College (http://www.dtic.mil/dtic/tr/fulltext/u2/a589335.pdf).

[16] Johnson, T. (2009). Ensuring the Success of Deploying Students: A Campus View. In R. Ackerman & D. DiRamio (Eds.), *Creating a Veteran-Friendly Campus: Strategies for Transition and Success* (55-60). New Directions for Student Services, 126. San Francisco: Jossey-Bass.

[17] Kleykamp, M. (2009). A great place to start? The effect of prior military service on hiring. *Armed Forces & Society*, 35(2), 266-285.

[18] Kleykamp, M. A. (2006). College, jobs, or the military? Enlistment during a time of war*. *Social Science Quarterly*, 87(2), 272-290.

[19] VOW To Hire Heroes Act (2011) *Public Law* 112-56,(http://npl.ly.gov.tw/pdf/7737.pdf

[20] Moon, T. L., & Schma, G. A. (2011). A proactive approach to serving military and veteran students. *New Directions for Higher Education*, 2011(153), 53-60.

[21] Morin, R. (2011). *The difficult transition from military to civilian life* Pew Research Center.

[22] Nowacek, R. S. (2011) *Agents of Integration*: Understanding Transfer as a Rhetorical Act. Carbondale: Southern Illinois UP.

[23] Taylor, P., ed. (2011) *The Military-Civilian Gap*: War and Sacrifice in the Post-9/11 Era. Washington, D.C.: Pew Research Center.

[24] Tuomi-Grohn, T., and Engestrom, Y. (2003) "Conceptualizing Transfer: From Standard Notions to Developmental Perspectives." In T. Tuomi-Grohn and Y. Engestrom. (Eds.), *Between Work and School: New Perspectives on Transfer and Boundary-Crossing*. (19-37). San Francisco: Pergamon.

[25] Turner, V. (1987). Betwixt and between: The liminal period in rites of passage. *Betwixt and between: Patterns of masculine and feminine initiation*, Open Court: La Salle, Illinois, pp. 5-22.

[26] Weaver, C. L. (2013). *Help wanted, help needed: Post 9/11 veteran's reintegration into the civilian labor market.* University of Texas at Austin, MA Thesis.

Preparing Skilled Veterans to Meet the Market and Growing Demand for Cybersecurity Talent

Richard Himmer, Mary A. Marks, John Adams Roach,
David Shaw, Wayne Washer

Abstract - Separating service members are a valuable pool of potential cybersecurity professionals.

Index Terms: Career Development, Education, Employment, Information Security

INTRODUCTION

By connecting the large pool of separating veterans to academic, government, industry and career transition partnerships, we can make great strides toward meeting the demand for cybersecurity talent. If we train even a modest percentage of separating service members in cybersecurity, it will go a long way towards filling the qualified cybersecurity talent gap.

The Need

A cursory search of the Internet reveals multiple studies, reports, and opinion pieces bemoaning the lack of qualified cybersecurity personnel.[1]

The Reinforcements

In response to the growing need for cybersecurity talent, we have a serendipitous surge in separating service members, as the military faces cutbacks.

---

[1] See, e.g.,www.rand.org/news/press/2014/06/18.html,
www.networkworld.com/article/2857305/cisco-subnet/cyber security-skills-shortage-panic-in-2015.html

The White House issued a 2013 report that noted the military expects to separate a million service members over the next several years.[2]

The Catalysts

To cover the need with reinforcements, there must be a catalyst to enable their successful merger. In this case, we have several.

Veterans have several advantages from their stint in the military that greatly increase their chances of successfully transitioning into the cybersecurity field.

A Veteran's background necessarily includes years of experience in general security, and often, robust opportunities for education and training, both while in the Service and after separation.

Over a third of our nation's military veterans have training in a variety of STEM disciplines. Another third or more receive technical training in weapon delivery systems and support systems that augment mission readiness. The military also trains a number of commissioned officers and enlisted personnel working in specific technical disciplines requiring advanced degrees, including PhDs.

Military Force Reductions

The 2015 Defense Department called for a reduction in active-duty military to 1.31 million troops, a decrease of nearly 37,000 service members from the previous year.

Defense Secretary Chuck Hagel called the reductions that eliminate an entire fleet of Air Force fighter planes and shrink the Army to its smallest size since before World War II "difficult choices." Hagel stated,

---

[2] http://www.whitehouse.gov/sites/default/files/docs/military_credentialing_and_licensing_report_2-24-2013_final.pdf

"These reductions will change defense institutions for years to come, but [are] designed to leave the military capable of fulfilling U.S. defense strategy and defending the homeland against strategic threats.[3]"

The military drawdown is moving highly trained and experienced men and women from the military to the private sector during one of the most challenging job markets since the great depression of 1929. The drawdown translates into an on-going challenge for our veterans in garnering paychecks after serving our nation valiantly.[4]

Veteran Unemployment

The jobless rate for retiring and separating military officers and enlisted personnel is almost 3% higher than civilians experience most likely due to the systematic challenges, veterans face systemic challenges in their transition to the private sector.

According to a 2014 RAND report, *"Between 2000 and 2011, younger veterans were, on average, 3.4 percentage points more likely to be unemployed than similarly situated younger non-veterans.[5]"*

---

[3] "Hagel Outlines Budget Reducing Troop Strength, Force Structure," DOD News Feb 24, 2014 by Nick Simeone, American Forces Press Service
[4] "CEO of Gallup calls jobless rate 'big lie' created by White House, Wall Street, media," February 05, 2015, FoxNews.com
[5] "Why Is Veteran Unemployment So High?" by David S. Loughran, Rand Corporation

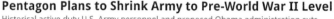

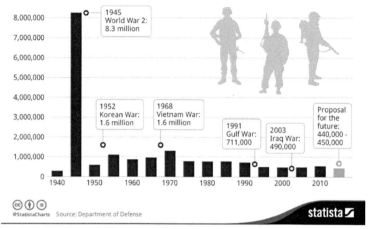

Pentagon Plans to Shrink Army to Pre-World War II Level

Historical active duty U.S. Army personnel and proposed Obama administration cuts

Source: Statista, Department of Defense

According to a 2013 article in Time Magazine, the primary issue is that today's business leaders do not understand the value that veterans bring to the table.

"This is one of the first generations of business leaders that largely didn't serve in the military, which poses real cultural barriers to understanding military skills and experience.[6]"

"One of the main barriers to hiring veterans, from the perspective of businesses, is that they struggle to understand how military skills translate to increasing the bottom line.[7]"

---

[6] "The Ground Truth on Veterans' Unemployment", Time, by Tom Tarantino, March 22, 2013

[7] Center for a New American Security, June 2012

In a 2012 survey of new veterans with Prudential, Inc., 60% of veterans reported that translating their military service to the civilian job market was a significant challenge.[8]

From our work, we have seen only modest improvement in this problem across the board. Although this situation is slowly improving, veterans still face frustration transitioning into the private sector.

While the military recently introduced a mandatory weeklong employment workshop, the Transition Assistance Program (TAP), which is helping to close the employment gap, it struggles to help executive-level veterans.[9]

MILITARY TRAINING AS A CATALYST FOR CYBERSECURITY CAREERS

While few military members have extensive training in computer science, all have a security mindset.

After highly publicized breaches of military networks, such as the Buckshot Yankee, WikiLeaks, and Snowden breaches, it was seen as an imperative that military members be vigilant with security of sensitive information.[10]

Required annual training has made all veterans aware of general cyber threats and threat actors. Almost all military members have held at least a Secret if not a Top Secret security clearance. Holding such a clearance means the veteran passed a thorough background check and was entrusted with information that would cause "serious damage" to national security if released.

To support the military, over one-third of our nation's military veterans have training in a variety of STEM disciplines.

---

[8] "The Ground Truth on Veterans' Unemployment," Time, by Tom Tarantino, March 22, 2013

[9] http://www.dol.gov/vets/programs/tap/

[10] See e.g., www.wired.com/tag/operation-buckshot-yankee/; www.reuters.com/article/2013/08/21/us-usa-wikileaks-manning-idUSBRE97J0JI20130821; http://www.thedailybeast.com/articles/2014/02/06/snowden-still-outwitting-u-s-spies.html

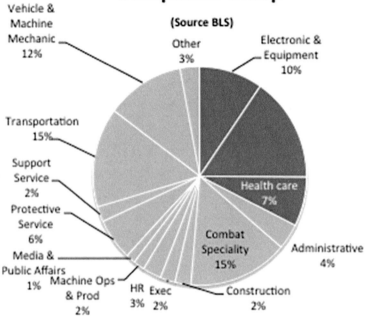

Source: Bureau of Labor Statistics

Another third or more receive technical training in weapon delivery systems and support systems that augment mission readiness. The military also trains a number of commissioned officers and enlisted personnel working in specific technical disciplines requiring advanced degrees, including Ph.Ds., through the military and a variety of post-graduate universities.

In addition, a number of our veterans work side by side with industry and government technical and scientific personnel on projects that allow them to gain deep cybersecurity subject matter expertise.

EDUCATIONAL OPPORTUNITIES AND THE GI BILL

Many of our veterans have the Montgomery GI Bill available for them to be retrained or enhance the skills that they currently have. Post-separation education can assist them in any skill mismatch engendered by military service. For example, according to Simon et al. (2009), almost one-third of enlisted veterans who separated between 1993 and 2000 made use of the Montgomery GI Bill benefits within the first two years of separation.

This is an opportunity to assist our exiting veterans to improve their skills and abilities by availing themselves of the benefits of the Montgomery GI Bill.

A critical area that many of these veterans can seek employment is in Science, Technology, Engineering, and Math (STEM) programs. Many of our post-secondary education systems are trying to attract our veterans into the STEM fields. There is a great need for many of our veterans to enter these fields to provide continued service and support to our nation. These needs were highlighted in a report to President Obama in 2012.

"Economic projections point to a need for approximately 1 million more STEM professionals than the U.S. will produce at the current rate over the next decade if the country is to retain its historical preeminence in science and technology. To meet this goal, the United States will need to increase the number of students who receive undergraduate STEM degrees by about 34% annually over current rates. Currently the United States graduates about 300,000 bachelor and associate degrees in STEM fields annually.[11]"

While separating service members may lack deep computer science backgrounds, almost all enlisted members and many officers have GI Bill benefits available to them. The GI Bill benefits will pay for certificate programs or even full four-year degrees in cybersecurity or other fields.[12]

Today, the Post-9/11 GI Bill benefits typically pay veterans a base salary and full tuition for 36 months of schooling. For veterans who have already completed some schooling before entering, or while serving in the military, the GI Bill can serve as a means to obtain a Master's degree or post-graduate certificates at no cost.

---

[11] Report to the President from The President's Council of Advisors on Science and Technology: Engage to Excel: Producing One Million Additional College Graduates with Degrees in Science, Technology, Engineering and Mathematics; Feb 2012

[12] http://www.military.com/education/gi-bill/new-post-911-gi-bill-overview.html

INDUSTRY OUTREACH

Other ways that we can encourage our exiting veterans to enter the STEM field is to have policies enacted that will focus on stimulating employer demand for veterans. For example, a variety of federal agencies facilitate the job search process through job fairs, online job search services (e.g., Department of Labor's CareerOneStop program), and facilitating connections between service members and employers before separation (e.g., Army Partnership for Youth Success [PaYS][13]). Explicit federal hiring preferences for disabled veterans and veterans of certain military operations as well as federal law barring discrimination against veterans (i.e., Uniformed Services Employment and Reemployment Rights Act) also operate on the demand side. The 2011 VOW to Hire Heroes Act includes a number of demand-side provisions, including tax credits for employers who hire veterans who have been unemployed for six months or more.

In addition to the robust education benefits available to many veterans, industry outreach is ubiquitous, enthusiastic, and well publicized.

Veteran jobs initiatives include the US Chamber of Commerce Foundation and Capital One's "Hiring 500,000 Heroes" program and JPMorgan Chase's "100,000 Jobs Mission." As their names imply, these are initiatives to hire 500,000 and 100,000 veterans respectively. Both programs met their goals ahead of schedule.[14] They have done this by encouraging hundreds of companies to commit to hiring veterans. Walmart, on its own, has committed to hiring 100,000 veterans over the next five years and made a pledge to hire any honorably discharged veteran.

The military has invested substantial time and energy into training Airmen, Soldiers, Sailors, and Marines to work hard in high-stress environments.

---

[13] https://www.armypays.com/INDEX.html

[14] http://www.uschamberfoundation.org/blog/post/hiring-our-heroes-capital-one-hit-major-milestone/42243; http://www.csrwire.com/press_releases/37673-100-000-Jobs-Mission-Hires-Over-200-000-Veterans

In essence, the military has pre-screened all applicants. In addition, by virtue of their honorable discharge, these veterans have demonstrated they are capable of performing at a satisfactory level in a rigorous job, and they have avoided misconduct and drug use.

Young separating veterans are in a position to go back to school and can take an entry-level job with a long productive future.

However, for executive-level members of the service, accustomed to compensation commensurate with their experience, starting back from square one is not a feasible option. To do so would be to leave their strongest attributes and work experience unutilized.

THE OUTLOOK FOR EXECUTIVE LEVEL VETERANS

When we look at the job market for senior-level officers and enlisted personnel who have served over 20 years and held jobs at high levels of leadership, the situation is more complex. Career military members have carried heavy responsibilities and may have made life-and-death decisions; often they have led dozens or hundreds of people and overseen multimillion-dollar programs. Some find jobs as civilians in the Department of Defense or hire on with a defense contractor.

However, once outside the defense arena, opportunities that can leverage their vast body of experience and provide comparable compensation are much more difficult to find. Even a position that requires leadership or managerial experience, which retiring officers have in spades, will additionally require intimate familiarity with the employer's field.

When looking more specifically at the growing field of cybersecurity, senior service members will need to capitalize on all that they have learned through the military.

While senior officers may lack deep technology skills[15], the military invests in training its workforce on cybersecurity.

Senior leaders, wherever they have served, are educated on the dangers of phishing and malware, cyber threat vectors, and the basics of information assurance and cybersecurity. They likely know more about cybersecurity than they think they do. They have also done risk management on a daily basis and have engaged in frequent exercises.

The military also invests in the latest technology, so members have worked with technological security devices, such as encrypted fiber optic connections, virtual private networks, two-factor authentication, and PKI certificates.

What brings this all together is formal, accredited coursework through education available locally and online. With some foresight, service members can easily complete their education before leaving the military. In addition, veterans can gain deeper, more specific and current knowledge of the latest cybersecurity trends by networking with professors and fellow students.

HELPING EXECUTIVE LEVEL VETERANS TRANSITION INTO CYBERSECURITY CAREERS

Virtually all veterans have received extensive training, many of them achieving graduate and advanced degrees, having taken advantage of the outstanding educational programs offered during their tenure of service. Almost 95% of senior officers have earned advanced degrees and over a third of senior enlisted have at least a bachelor's degree.[16]

In addition, such training has not been offered solely to commissioned officers. Forbes contributor Shaun So asked the rhetorical question, *"Should a prior service enlisted veteran with both bachelors and masters degrees be passed over a leadership career path because they're enlisted?"* He continued:

---

[15] Senior officers from the class of 1990 were pre-World Wide Web and likely never took more than a typing course before entering the military.
[16] http://www.afpc.af.mil/library/airforcepersonneldemographics.asp

Today's soldiers, regardless of their ranks, are trained in some of the world's most elite leadership courses. Furthermore, they are battle tested and capable of accomplishing seemingly impossible tasks, again, regardless of their rank. Yes, there are distinct differences between enlisted and officer leadership roles, however, I do not think that those differences should prevent an enlisted veteran candidate from future corporate leadership training opportunities. [17]

GLOBAL BUSINESS RESOURCES MILITARY TRANSITION PROCESS

Following the service drawdown from the Vietnam War, and despite extensive leadership experience and solid educational credentials one of the authors struggled in the job market. Because of this personal experience, he started a company in 1983 to focus on career counseling and placement for mid- to upper-level executives. With multiple offices, the company quickly grew into a significant player in the employment industry and surpassed industry averages for placement of executives into the marketplace.

Over the years of operation, the company pioneered innovative and exciting processes for successfully helping men and women of all ages and backgrounds, including veterans, enter the job market. We also provided consulting services for businesses and seminars and classes for career-centered applicants seeking advancement.

For the past 30 years, volatile changes in the job market, advances in supporting technologies, and our unique underlying knowledge base have driven us to re-energize our employment services under our not-for-profit company, Global Business Resources (GBR).

GBR provides multiple resources for the veteran job seeker along with people who provide philosophical support in terms of research and concepts that are essential ingredients of our success equation.

---

[17] http://www.forbes.com/sites/oracle/2015/02/09/how-your-organization-can-avoid-an-integration-debacle/

We have found that using a multi-step process is a best practice in assisting veterans with accurately translating their military experiences into understandable skills that are recognized and valued by private sector hiring managers. These steps include:

1) Career Assessment with an expanded personal assessment process emphasizing skills analysis and transference. A part of this process is for the veteran to assess accurately and understand their skill sets developed from both experience and training during their service tenure. The challenge for the veteran is articulating these skills and abilities into meaningful and understandable civilian-equivalent skills. For those with fewer technical skills and training, a steeper challenge is how to leverage this training as a catalyst for transitioning into the private sector.

2) Mentoring and coaching are key ingredients for success in this continuously evaluated process. The mentor's role is to help the veteran as a skills translator. A mentor must understand the private sector and the wide range of the skills fostered by military training to successfully aid the veteran's transition. The mentor also needs to have an intimate knowledge of the various technical educational opportunities available to the veteran.

3) Market research to ensure we are staying in tune with market signals and making any adjustments to benefit the veteran client.

4) Self-employment workshops for veterans who prefer to establish and control their career paths. For certain technologies, product incubators are conducted to assist the veteran in the most difficult challenge of all, producing a successful business entity.

5) Soft skills development, including Emotional Intelligence training.

USING EMOTIONAL INTELLIGENCE IN THE MILITARY TRANSITION PROCESS

Transitioning is a challenge that besets all human beings. Growing up in a military household, one is forced to transition into new schools, communities, churches, and ball teams. Some learn the necessary adaptation skills. For those who do not, they dread the process and are filled with anxiety.

For military personnel who already have gainful employment, going through the final months of service is a formality filled with trepidation of having to color-coordinate what they wear to work post military life. To those without secure employment, life outside of military service can be filled with anxiety, wondering how finances will work and how to handle the day-to-day routine no longer regulated by the government.

Another concern is the civilian spouse who is accustomed to running the household in the absence of his/her military significant other. The family dynamics will be disrupted upon the veteran's return. Determining how the roles will be filled is as challenging as finding new employment.

Research in the field of Emotional Intelligence (EI) has found that up to 20% of a person's overall success in life is IQ or technical skills related compared to 47% of their overall success that is directly related to social skills.[18]

EI is defined as *"a set of emotional and social skills that influence the way we perceive and express ourselves, develop and maintain social relationships, cope with challenges, and use emotional information in an effective and meaningful way.*[19]"

People with high EI are skilled at specific emotional competencies and have learned social capabilities that result in outstanding work performance.[20]

In a study called the GLOBE Project, a study conducted by 160 social scientists that examined the interrelationships of societal and organizational cultures and organizational leadership.[21] They studied 60 cultures, which represented all of the major regions of the world and they found that EI transcended cultures, nations, and politics. The GLOBE Project highlighted that EI is not just a U.S. fad or a culturally indigenous belief structure (House,

---

[18] Stein & Book, 2011
[19] Multi Health Systems, 2013, p. 2
[20] Goleman, 1998
[21] As reported by House, 1998

1998). Dysfunctional personality characteristics often are hidden from view when considering employees through the lens of technical or cognitive skills.[22]

The US Air Force used the EI-i assessment to select recruiters found the ability to predict successful recruiters increased by three fold.[23] Their immediate gain was $3 million annually. When the data was submitted to the Government Accounting Office (GAO), the Secretary of Defense ordered all branches of the armed forces to adopt the EI process for recruiters.

Research by the Center for Creative Leadership found that the primary cause executives become derailed are deficits in emotional competency. The three top EI skills that suffer are change management, team dynamics, and interpersonal relationships.[24]

Supervisors in a large manufacturing plant were given training in EI competencies such as listening and problem solving. After the training,

- Lost-time accidents were reduced by 50%

- Formal grievances were reduced from 15% per year to 3% per year

- Plant exceeded productivity goals by $250,000[25]

Porras and Anderson conducted a similar study with supervisory training.[26] Production increased 17% when supervisors were given EI training compared to no increase for supervisors not given EI training.

Introducing EI training to transitioning soldiers will not only aid in their search for gainful employment but also increase the probability of keeping their family relations intact.[27] EI has shown to enhance the probability of a happier marriage and introducing EI into parenting increases the probability of children having the social skills necessary to cope with their daily challenges.[28]

---

[22] Nelson & Hogan, 2009
[23] Cherniss, 1999
[24] Cherniss, 1999
[25] Pesuric & Byham, 1996
[26] Porras and Anderson, 1981
[27] Gottman, 2002; Gottman & Silver, 1999
[28] Gottman & DeClaire, 1998

SUMMARY

Our country depends on the future of our promising military veteran leaders.

Academia, Government, and Industry must do everything they can to court and nurture veterans regardless of their rank, because, to quote Shaun So again, leadership is, "a process of social influence in which one person can enlist the aid and support of others in the accomplishment of a common task.

What is the only prerequisite? Being a person. Everything else is gravy.[29]"

Do these biases continue to persist? Yes, and in an ever-wider swath within the private hiring sector as more and more veterans are released into the job market. We agree with Mr. So's contribution and firmly disagree with these career segregation policies. However, this problem has been persistent for several decades and will not be solved anytime soon.

For this reason, rather than attack the system, we advocate a leveling of the perception of veterans' qualifications by setting the stage for a new and exciting career path. We can transition veterans' military careers into cybersecurity careers by connecting academic opportunities, the government, and industry. Such efforts will level the playing field for skilled talent while opening up new and exciting cybersecurity careers paths for veterans.

Our veterans already have significant STEM skills, training, experience, and expertise, and have earned the right to update and certify their knowledge to meet private sector employment opportunities. Though this concept makes sense at a macro level, each case is unique and competent execution will require one-on-one counseling and mentorship that takes into account the multiple variables of each veteran's situation.

---

[29] http://www.forbes.com/sites/oracle/2015/02/09/how-your-organization-can-avoid-an-integration-debacle/

ABOUT GBR

GBR is associated with the University of Washington Tacoma Center for Information Assurance and Cybersecurity. Several programs are offered by the Center of Excellence that provides undergraduate and graduate programs along with certifications in risk assurance and cybersecurity.

Our program is but one tool for the veteran to amplify skills and use military training as a catalyst for accomplishing a successful transition into valuable and rewarding cybersecurity careers in the private sector.

REFERENCES

[1] Cherniss, C. (1999). The business case for emotional intelligence. *Consortium for Research on Emotional Intelligence in Organizations*, 4, 5.

[2] Goleman, D. (1998). *Working with emotional intelligence.* Retrieved from http://books.google.com/

[3] Goleman, D. (2005). *Emotional intelligence.* New York, NY: Bantam Books.

[4] Gottman, J. (2002). *The Relationship Cure: A 5 Step Guide to Strengthening Your Marriage, Family, and Friendships.* Three Rivers Press.

[5] Gottman, J., & DeClaire, J. (1998). *Raising an emotionally intelligent child.* New York, N.Y.: Simon & Schuster.

[6] Gottman, J., & Silver, N. (1999). *The Seven Principles for Making Marriage Work: A Practical Guide from the Country's Foremost Relationship Expert* (1ST ed.). Crown.

[7] House, R. J. (1998). A brief history of GLOBE. *Journal of Managerial Psychology*, 13(3-4), 230–240. doi:10.1108/02683949810215048

[8] Multi Health Systems. (2013). *EQ user's handbook.* MHS. Retrieved from ei.mhs.com/

[9] Nelson, E., & Hogan, R. (2009). Coaching on the Dark Side. *International Coaching Psychology Review*, 4(1), 9–21.

[10] Pesuric, A., & Byham, W. (1996). The new look in behavior modeling. *Training and Development*, 25–33.

[11] Porras, J. I., & Anderson, B. (1981). Improving managerial effectiveness through modeling-based training. *Organizational Dynamics*, 9(4), 60–77.

[12] Stein, S. J., & Book, H. E. (2011). *The EQ edge: Emotional intelligence and your success*. Mississauga, ON: Jossey-Bass.

Re-Engineering the Cybersecurity Human Capital Crisis

Morgan Zantua, Marc Dupuis, Barbara Endicott-Popovsky

University of Washington Tacoma

Abstract - The demand for cybersecurity professionals continues to significantly outpace the supply with a projected worldwide shortage of two million by 2017. At the same time, there are large numbers of transitioning military personnel that have important technical skills that could be coalesced into addressing this demand. This paper examines the development and proposed deployment of a project to do just this: Cybersecurity Rapid Education Apprenticeship Training to Employment System (CREATES). Challenges and benefits are discussed.

Keywords: transitioning military personnel, cybersecurity supply and demand, veterans, training

INTRODUCTION

While our nation's infrastructure is vulnerable to cyber-attack and cyber misuse, there is a critical deficit of cybersecurity professionals to address the problem (Burley, Eisenberg, & Goodman, 2014). Thousands of career positions in information assurance and cybersecurity are going unfilled (Conklin, Cline, & Roosa, 2014; Cranor L.F. & Sadeh N., 2013). Yet, the demand is only going to continue to increase to unprecedented levels. A report by the United Kingdom's House of Lords indicates a worldwide shortage of two million cybersecurity professionals by 2017 (Oltsik, 2014).

At the same time the military drawdown is releasing personnel with intensive technical training, often in the computing sciences (Mitcham, 2013; Soldan, Schulz, Gruenbacher, Vogt, & Natarajan, 2011). These veterans could leverage their background with appropriate academic education in information assurance (IA) and cybersecurity to fill the country's need for IA professionals.

This paper briefly explains the background of the problem, an approach to address the problem, and how this approach can later be refined and disseminated to other interested entities for maximum impact. Ultimately, the goal is to leverage our transitioning military personnel to address the severe shortage of cybersecurity professionals. This approach will serve as a win–win–win with direct benefits for veterans, public organizations, and the private sector.

BACKGROUND

The Center for Information Assurance Cybersecurity (CIAC), housed at the Provost's office at the University of Washington and encompassing the University of Hawaii, is an incubator for cutting edge research in Information Assurance (IA) curricula development. Since 2007, Endicott-Popovsky and Popovsky's initial research has developed:

- 107 students earning a certificate in IA
- 40 Masters of Science in Info. Management students with a concentration in IA
- 4 Masters of Library and Information Science students with a concentration in IA
- 76 students receiving a Master of Strategic Planning in Critical Infrastructure
- 26 Master's in Cybersecurity and Leadership
- 8 PhD students across all disciplines, with an IA focus

In 2012, Dr. Endicott-Popovsky's Information Security Risk Management (ISRM) curriculum was offered on Coursera. Over 50,000 students globally enrolled in the free ISRM 10-week course.

Based on the track record of the CIAC, it was awarded a two-year grant called VetsEngr in 2010 (NSF award EEC-1037814). The purpose of the grant was to conduct case studies of returning veterans to determine the feasibility of transitioning these individuals into cybersecurity roles through appropriate education in information assurance. As a result of this initial study, NIST recently awarded a one-year bridge grant to lay the foundation of a model within Washington State to guide National Guard, Reservists, and transitioning military into public two- and four-year cybersecurity-related programs.

The model, Cybersecurity Rapid Education Apprenticeship Training to Employment System (CREATES), builds a pipeline, with on and off ramps, throughout the network of two-year associate degrees, four-year college and university degrees, certificates, masters, and doctoral degrees. In the first phase of the grant a database will provide a complete guide to education resources within Washington State. A companion guide to over 180 NIETP Centers of Academic Excellence and Research in Information Assurance will be made available to military transitioning out of Washington.

The question becomes how to identify those most suited to this profession. The initial pilot participants were highly selected volunteers initially interested in a digital forensics class. Candidates were interviewed, assessed to determine background in computer technology, and culled through to determine verbal and mathematical aptitudes. This resource intensive process relied heavily upon candidates knowing enough about Cybersecurity/Information Assurance to have an interest in Digital Forensics.

Could a broader range of individuals do equally well? And how can the candidates most likely to succeed be identified? If we want to increase the numbers we serve, and we certainly need to, then we must develop an efficient process to identify candidates with "the right stuff" to succeed in the ubiquitous and interdisciplinary cybersecurity field.

THE PROBLEM

The Department of Labor, Bureau of Labor Statistics reports a 37% increase in security analysts since 2012 and projects continued demand for individuals with this skill set (Bureau of Labor Statistics, 2014). Amazon, Microsoft, and other major companies pay top dollar for American talent and continue to import talent from around the globe to supplement their cybersecurity workforce (Fourie et al., 2014). Government agencies (city, county, state and federal) have the same gaps in filling their workforce needs (Paulsen C., McDuffie E., Newhouse W., & Toth P., 2012).

This study will link the demand side of the burgeoning cybersecurity workforce with the supply side coming from the transitioning military community. The supply side for cybersecurity professionals has been a major impediment to addressing the shortage and this is one way to bridge that gap (Wilson & Ali, 2011). Additionally, one major economic challenge facing the Department of Defense is the high cost of unemployment benefits being paid out to transitioning service members (Kleykamp, 2013). This project will help address this economic challenge as well.

Imagine a proactive methodology used to identify high potential cybersecurity professionals early in the military transition process. Regardless of the Army's Military Occupational Status, Air Force Specialty Code, or the Navy's rating, talent can be identified and moved into the CREATES pipeline in anticipation of transitioning out of the military and into government or private sector cybersecurity careers.

CHALLENGES, BENEFITS, AND PROPOSED APPROACH

Conducting this research with the military provides both short- and long-term benefits. The military represents a diverse population for this study, especially with respect to ethnic diversity (Lundquist, 2008). And as discussed earlier and studied in the VetsEngr grant, today's military receive state-of-the-art technical training; yet few move forward utilizing their GI Bill to leverage this experience into academic pathways enabling them access to higher paying cybersecurity positions in government and industry.

Likewise, those that do utilize their GI Bill often choose community colleges or for-profit colleges rather than universities, such as state or private not-for-profit universities (Field, Hebel, & Smallwood, 2008). This is due primarily to the convenience provided by community colleges and for-profit entities, as well as the greater likelihood that transitioning military personnel will receive credit for training they received while on active duty. In the process, students may be limiting their options and eventual career opportunities, such as cybersecurity.

This research will examine a broader base of individuals for cybersecurity careers and will incorporate frameworks based on complementary efforts from entities such as NIST (Paulsen C. et al., 2012). The initiative will generate awareness and move more individuals into the CREATES pipeline. The assessment tool will be 'beta tested' on transitioning military and reserve components. As the tool is refined, it can be utilized on a larger pool of candidates and help them to enter the cybersecurity field to address the shortage of cybersecurity professionals in the workforce. A longitudinal study will examine the long-term impact of assessment upon the military transitioning: their career choice within cybersecurity, wage progression, and professional development.

CONCLUSION

Developing an accessible assessment tool and replicating the CREATES model will do more than address the initial shortage of cybersecurity professionals. For example, it will be able to help combat the lack of female representation in the cybersecurity field, which has been a significant issue resulting in a deficit of diversity in viewpoints (Dampier, Kelly, & Carr, 2012).

Additionally, the tool will be a resource provided to several different entities. For example, the CIAC proposes to introduce the assessment tool to academic organizations and K-12 systems throughout the CIAC network of NIETP Academic Centers of Excellence and professional organizations such as IEEE, University Professional Continuing Educator Association (UPCEA), Cyberwatch, Colloquium Information Security Systems Education (CISSE), NIST, and the Council of College and Military Educators (CMEC).

On October 4, 1957 Sputnik changed the course of American education for the next two decades and subsequently built a strong technical workforce that kept America at the forefront of the space race and technological innovation (Wissehr, Concannon, & Barrow, 2011).

September 11th, this generation's wake-up call, brought a renewed patriotism to many who chose to protect and defend their country (Poulin, Silver, Gil-Rivas, Holman, & McIntosh, 2009; Sahar, 2008). Development and utilization of this assessment tool and the instantiation of CREATES provides an opportunity to harness the talent and patriotism of this generation to proactively protect and defend our nation against an impending Cyber 9/11.

REFERENCES

[1] Bureau of Labor Statistics. (2014). *Information Security Analysts*. U.S. Department of Labor. Retrieved from http://www.bls.gov/ooh/computer-and-information-technology/information-security-analysts.htm

[2] Burley, D. L., Eisenberg, J., & Goodman, S. E. (2014). Would cybersecurity professionalization help address the cybersecurity crisis? *Commun.* ACM, 57(2), 24–27.

[3] Conklin, W. A., Cline, R. E., & Roosa, T. (2014). Re-engineering Cybersecurity Education in the US: An Analysis of the Critical Factors. System Sciences (HICSS), *2014 47th Hawaii International Conference on*, 2006–2014. doi:10.1109/HICSS.2014.254

[4] Cranor L.F., & Sadeh N. (2013). A shortage of privacy engineers. *IEEE Secur. Privacy IEEE Security and Privacy*, 11(2), 77–79.

[5] Dampier, D., Kelly, K., & Carr, K. (2012). Increasing Participation of Women in Cyber Security. In *ASEE-SE Regional Conference*, Starkville, MS.

[6] Field, K., Hebel, S., & Smallwood, S. (2008). Cost, convenience drive veterans' college choices. *Chronicle of Higher Education*, 54(46), A1–A14.

[7] Fourie, L., Pang, S., Kingston, T., Hettema, H., Watters, P., & Sarrafzadeh, H. (2014). The global cyber security workforce: an ongoing human capital crisis. *Global Business and Technology Association.*

[8] Kleykamp, M. (2013). Unemployment, earnings and enrollment among post 9/11 veterans. *Social Science Research*, 42(3), 836–851. doi:10.1016/j.ssresearch.2012.12.017

[9] Lundquist, J. H. (2008). Ethnic and Gender Satisfaction in the Military: The Effect of a Meritocratic Institution. *American Sociological Review*, 73(3), 477–496.

[10] Mitcham, M. (2013). Academic Recognition of Military Experience in STEM Education. *American Council on Education.*

[11] Oltsik, J. (2014, December 9). Cybersecurity Skills Shortage Panic in 2015? Retrieved from http://www.networkworld.com/article/2857305/cisco-subnet/cybersecurity-skills-shortage-panic-in-2015.html

[12] Paulsen C., McDuffie E., Newhouse W., & Toth P. (2012). NICE: Creating a cybersecurity workforce and aware public. *IEEE Secur. Privacy IEEE Security and Privacy*, 10(3), 76–79.

[13] Poulin, M. J., Silver, R. C., Gil-Rivas, V., Holman, E. A., & McIntosh, D. N. (2009). Finding social benefits after a collective trauma: Perceiving societal changes and well-being following 9/11. *Journal of Traumatic Stress*, 22(2), 81–90. doi:10.1002/jts.20391

[14] Sahar, G. (2008). Patriotism, Attributions for the 9/11 Attacks, and Support for War: Then and Now. *Basic and Applied Social Psychology*, 30(3), 189–197. doi:10.1080/01973530802374956

[15] Soldan, D. L., Schulz, N. N., Gruenbacher, D. M., Vogt, B. M., & Natarajan, R. (2011). Work in progress - Streamlining pathways to engineering degrees for military veterans. *Frontiers in Education Conference (FIE)*, 2011, F3J–1. doi:10.1109/FIE.2011.6142736

[16] Wilson, A., & Ali, A. (2011). The Biggest Threat to the U.S. Digital Infrastructure: The Cyber Security Workforce Supply Chain. *Academy for Studies in Business*, 3(2), 15.

[17] Wissehr, C., Concannon, J., & Barrow, L. H. (2011). Looking Back at the Sputnik Era and Its Impact on Science Education. *School Science & Mathematics*, 111(7), 368–375.

Systems Thinking Pedagogical Design: Developing a Veteran–Centric Masters Degree In Cybersecurity and Leadership

Tracy Thompson, Marc Dupuis, Bryan Goda, Yan Bai, Charles Costarella, Morgan Zantua

University of Washington Tacoma

Abstract - Cybersecurity is a promising area because business, military, government, and utilities all desire trained cybersecurity professionals that can lead and effect change. Post-9/11 veterans represent a large untapped pool of talent ideal for addressing the nation's shortage of senior cyber leaders. But veterans often have difficulty transitioning to the civilian workforce. If they are to take advantage of the opportunity to usher military veterans into careers as cybersecurity leaders, universities need to engage in systems thinking pedagogical design. This paper introduces and assesses the utility of one approach for design as suggested by the KBP Pedagogical Model (Endicott-Popovsky & Popovsky, 2014). We use UW Tacoma's experience in mounting a new Master's level degree program in Cybersecurity and Leadership (the MCL) as a test case to evaluate the utility of this model for developing a veteran-centric approach to cyber security education. A retrospective analysis reveals the model to provide a useful frame for how to design the content of the curriculum and how it should be taught, but that it should be extended to address additional elements at the organizational level. Mechanisms to ensure strong and ongoing structural linkages between university schools support the interdisciplinary nature of the curriculum, control systems in the form of ongoing curricular evaluations methods support ongoing learning and the deep incorporation of non-faculty recruiting and advising capabilities into the administrative organization supports the students and ongoing ability of the faculty to adjust and deliver the curriculum. Each of these organizational design elements are critical features that enhance the performance of the pedagogical system and lower the risk of developing a new degree program that serves the needs of the transitioning veteran.

INTRODUCTION

Post-9/11 veterans, especially members of the officer corps who possess four-year or advanced college degrees, represent a large pool of untapped talent ideal for addressing the nation's shortage in the engineering and science workforce (Report of the National Science Foundation Workshop on Enhancing the Post-9/11 Veterans Educational Benefit, 2009). Demand for cybersecurity personnel continues to increase (Gjelton, 2010) and senior cyber leaders who can effectively communicate cyber-related business cases and are able to lead, persuade, and negotiate in a fast-moving business environment are in particularly scarce supply (CSFI, 2014; Roman, 2012). Many of those who serve today and are looking to transition out of the military are experienced in managing technical systems, solving complex problems, and leading teams. But these veterans often have difficulty translating their skills into the civilian work world, adjusting to a more individualistic and unstructured work environment, and engaging in effective job searches (Simpson & Armstrong, 2009; Stone & Stone, 2014). Capitalizing on this opportunity to develop and shape post 9-11 veterans into workforce-ready cybersecurity professionals requires educational institutions to develop specialized degree programs at the Masters level.

However, the startup of any new Master's program can be a risky proposition, especially one that will serve our nation's veterans. Basic questions need to be answered about the local context facing a proposed program, including: "Who will attend this program? What is the demand for this program? What skills should graduates have? Who will hire them after they leave the program? How should the curriculum be designed?"

One way to begin to addressing these questions is to employ a holistic model that can guide design efforts. This paper introduces and assesses the utility of one approach for design as suggested by the KBP Pedagogical Model (Endicott-Popovsky & Popovsky, 2014). We use UW Tacoma's experience in mounting a new Master's level degree program in Cybersecurity and Leadership (the MCL) as a test case to evaluate the utility of this model for developing a new veteran-centric approach to cyber security education. Our retrospective analysis reveals the model to provide a useful frame for designing the curriculum itself but it also points to the importance of considering the organizational context within which curriculum resides. In particular, curriculum exists inside universities as organizations, and our work highlights the importance of how the curriculum needs to be supported by additional organizational design elements. Mechanisms to ensure strong and ongoing structural linkages between university schools support the interdisciplinary nature of the curriculum, control systems in the form of ongoing curricular evaluations methods support ongoing learning, and the deep incorporation of non-faculty recruiting and advising capabilities into the administrative organization supports the students and ongoing ability of the faculty to adjust and deliver the curriculum. Each of these organizational design elements are critical features that enhance the performance of the pedagogical system and lower the risk of developing a new degree program that serves the needs of the transitioning veteran.

APPLYING THE KBP MODEL TO UW TACOMA'S MCL PROGRAM

Figure 1 provides an overview of the KBP Pedagogical Model (Endicott-Popovsky & Popovsky, 2014) which offers a systems view of curriculum development. In such a system, resources (potential students), the job market, and trends in the larger societal and economic environment are inputs. New students are transformed via an educational process into outputs, in this case professionals. The internal components related to the model consist of two human elements, students and teachers, and three infrastructure elements, the goals, content, and didactic processes of the curriculum (see Figure 1). Congruence, or the notion of fit, underpins the model – when the elements fit together, the inputs (veteran students) transform into the desired outcomes, in this case, cybersecurity professionals with leadership capability. The model is also dynamic, so as any one element changes over time, other elements need to be adjusted to maintain good fit and hence performance.

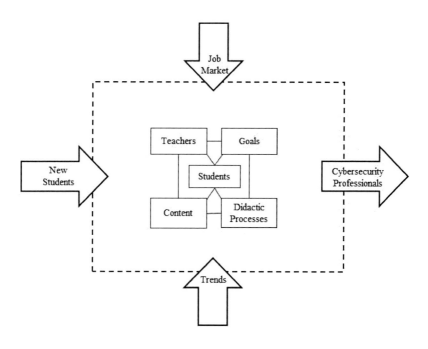

Figure 1. KBP Pedagogical Model for IA Curriculum Development

Students are at the heart of the KBP model; for purposes of our analysis we examine the fits between veterans as students and the other elements of the model. After providing a brief overview of UW Tacoma's MCL degree program, we evaluate the local context and opportunity, focusing on the supply of potential students, the demand for jobs, and the trends in the competitive context. Collectively, these factors shape the curriculum, specifically, the program learning goals, the teachers, the content of the curriculum, and the didactic processes. After explaining how these elements are designed to fit together in order to integrate technical and business concerns and to serve veterans seeking to become future cybersecurity leaders, we highlight additional organizational design factors that supplement the KBP model.

INPUTS: THE STUDENTS, THE JOB MARKET AND TRENDS IN THE MARKETPLACE

Founded in 1990, the University of Washington Tacoma (UWT) campus is located approximately 10 miles from Joint Base Lewis-McChord, one of the premier military installations on the West Coast. The opportunity for a Cybersecurity and Leadership program at the graduate level was supported by a strong local source of students, strong demand by employers, and a lack of competitors in the region. Approached by the Washington National Guard who wanted to have a professional degree program that would support their mission to respond to cybersecurity attacks on our nation's infrastructure, the Institute of Technology and the Milgard School of Business began to explore a joint degree program in 2012 (Goda & Friedman, 2012). The degree program is highly interdisciplinary in nature. It combines a technological education in cybersecurity policy and design with managerial and leadership skills yielding graduates who are well-positioned to lead an organization's cybersecurity functions and to advocate for the role that cybersecurity plays in furthering an organization's performance and effectiveness.

UWT's proximity to the Army and Air Force at JBLM and the Washington Air and Army National Guard provide an excellent source of students, the first contextual element in the KBP Model. Moreover, JBLM is surrounded by a veteran rich population (1 out of every 11 citizens in Washington State is a veteran). The U.S. Military's continued drawdown from its Iraq War peak strength has and will continue to strongly affect the South Puget Sound region, with some estimating JBLM to lose as many as 11,000 positions (Ashton, 2014, 2015). Outside of the military, the South Puget Sound and the I-5 corridor around UWT is home to such tech savvy companies as Microsoft, Amazon, Boeing, Liberty Mutual, Pacific Medical Centers, KPMG, and the Port of Tacoma, all of whom are likely to supply students to the program. Thus, market conditions suggest a strong supply of new students to feed the program.

A second contextual input into the KBP Pedagogical Model is the job market. This contextual element drives demand and shapes the desired goals and content of a program. In case of cybersecurity professionals, healthy demand exists at the national level for middle- to senior-level leaders of cybersecurity (CSFI, 2014; Gjelten, 2010; Roman, 2012). At the local level, the aforementioned tech savvy and large employers suggest a similar condition. In addition, when asked to go on record to support the development of the MCL program, several UW Tacoma constituents such as the Institute of Technology Advisory Board, the Milgard School of Business Advisory Board, local business leaders, and government agencies all indicated great enthusiasm and interest for the program, saying they would hire these graduates.

An additional input that was considered at the time the program was being proposed relates to the trends in the external marketplace. In addition to the clear demand for cybersecurity professionals with managerial and leadership expertise, the economics and competitive landscape facing UWT revealed a clear market opportunity for this type of program, particularly on the West Coast. An informal benchmarking exercise in 2012-2013 revealed a number of online and resident master degrees in cybersecurity housed in computer science departments. Of note, the exercise found only a few programs that combined business leadership courses with cybersecurity courses, and none located on the West coast.[1]

These efforts to understand the supply of potential students in the local area, particularly those coming from the military, and the demand conditions in terms of the job market and the competitive landscape, mitigate the risk this new program. But more importantly, per the KBP model, they also shape the curricular design. After identifying the specific needs of veterans transitioning to the civilian workplace, we describe the MCL program in terms of its goals, teachers, curriculum content, and didactic processes and explain how each of these elements integrates cybersecurity with business in a way that uniquely serves transitioning military personnel. We also highlight how additional organizational and administrative elements also enable and improve the

---

[1] Example of graduate programs that combine technical skills with leadership skills include the National Defense University's Government Information Leadership Masters Degree, George Mason University's Masters in Management of Secure Information Systems, George Washington University's World Executive MBA in Cybersecurity, and Washington University's Cybersecurity Management (c.f., CSFI, 2014).

program's interdisciplinary content and it's responsiveness to the veteran student population.

VETERANS AND MCL CURRICULUM DESIGN

Veterans have difficulty translating their skills into the civilian work world, adjusting to a different workplace culture, and engaging in effective job searches (Simpson & Armstrong, 2009; Stone & Stone, 2014). Identifying relevant skills learned in the military and translating them in ways that are meaningful in civilian organizations can be overwhelming to veterans (Biggs, 2014). In addition, veterans report culture shock and the shift from regimented, hierarchical, and a more group oriented environment to a more unstructured environment that focuses on individuality is a big concern (Simpson & Armstrong, 2009). Frequent relocation means that veterans are typically not well connected or networked in the civilian world (Clemens & Milson, 2008), and the skill and processes associated with meeting others, looking for and interviewing for jobs also presents challenges (Biggs, 2014; Simpson & Armstrong, 2009). The main elements of the MCL program, including the mix of students accepted into the program, the learning goals of the program, the content of the curriculum, the mix of teachers, and the didactic processes used in the classes all help the military veteran overcome these challenges and transition successfully into cybersecurity careers in the civilian workplace.

Students

The mix of incoming students is one factor that helps veterans transition. Rather than being just for veterans, the MCL is designed for both military and non-military students. The program also selects individuals with both a technical background in network design and substantial work experience (military work counts as work experience). Although it is a full time program, the MCL program accommodates students who are normally working during the day. Full-time status enables MCL students to qualify for Veteran's and active duty funding. This combined with an evening delivery model allows the program to meet the needs of military personnel anticipating a transition to the private sector, veterans, retirees as well as others from the private and government sectors. Students attend classes two nights a week, with only small parts of some courses being offered online. Nearly 60% of the first two cohorts of MCL students are military-related, including Active Duty, Reserves, National Guard, veterans, and retirees, with the remaining coming from the governmental and private sectors.

Program Goals

The overarching goal of the MCL program is to produce students who will understand the design and policy issues surrounding cybersecurity and be able to solve problems, manage people, information, and processes to accomplish broader organizational and business goals related to cybersecurity. Table 2 lists the four specific learning objectives of the MCL Program. These learning objectives serve both veterans who are not fluent in the language and practices of business as well as technical types who may not be attuned to the organizational and behavioral sides of management.

1) **Communication Skills:** Our graduates are fluent interdisciplinary communicators who can integrate the technical aspects of cybersecurity with the strategic and managerial concerns of their organization.

2) **Risk Management Skills:** Our graduates are diagnostic problem-solvers who can evaluate the information security needs and design strong cybersecurity capabilities into their organization. Our students are able to use risk assessment concepts and methodologies to determine proactive measures in protecting their organization from critical data exposure, and they are able to evaluate a major cybersecurity event, evaluate the business impact, determine a risk posture, and develop effective responses.

3) **Leadership and Interpersonal Skills:** Our graduates are change-savvy managers who can effectively coordinate activities and lead individuals and teams. They know how to launch and assess organizational

change initiatives, understand how to effectively lead and manage teams, and they can work effectively within an interdependent group to achieve common goals.

Table 1. Program Learning Objectives for the MCL

Content and Teachers

The content of the MCL curriculum is delivered as a traditional program with resident instruction and is structured on a cohort basis where students take a locked sequence of courses together. The cohort design with lock-step classes helps to develop a strong culture and supportive network among students in the program. Connections that form between those with a military and those without a military background help the transitioning veteran connect his experience to the outside business world. In terms of the class content itself, on the technical side, the MCL program exposes students to the principles of data protection, network security, counter cyber-terrorist techniques, and risk management. And on the managerial side, the MCL program gives students the perspective and understanding of an organizational leader that extends beyond the IT function so that they can effectively advocate for cybersecurity issues at the highest levels of the organization.

The curriculum content consists of eight 5-credit courses which are designed and taught by faculty from the Institute of Technology and the Milgard School of Business. Two classes are offered each quarter for a total of 40 credits, and in any given quarter, students have one class taught by a professor from the Milgard School and the other taught by a professor from the Institute of Technology. The content and flow of the classes listed below have been designed to expose the transitioning veteran (and the technical employee who may be siloed in the IT function) to see the bigger picture of business. All of the courses focus on preparing the student to work on a team solving a capstone cybersecurity project in a real organization.

Autumn Quarter (Introduction)	*Principles of Cybersecurity* provides an overview of the ten domains of cybersecurity.
	Business Essentials provides an overview of key concepts in business including business communication, marketing, ethics, accounting, and financial analysis.
Winter Quarter	*Information Assurance, Risk Management, and Security Strategies* exposes students to key risk assessment and management frameworks, which enables them to assess and prioritize risk in an organizational setting and communicate these risks to high level decision makers.
	Individual and Group Dynamics prepares students to establish, manage, and lead high-performing, successful teams and to lead their own careers effectively.
Spring Quarter	*Network and Internet Security* ensures that students are exposed to current industry best practices, such as white listing, intrusion detection systems, and other technical and policy concepts. Additionally, students are exposed to concepts in high demand by governmental organizations, such as defense in depth, constant monitoring, and incident response preparedness.
	Strategic Organizational Change explores the repertoire of concepts, tools, and techniques for understanding the strategic management of organizations and how successful leaders and change agents can create, implement, and manage change.

Summer Quarter (Capstone)	*Cybersecurity Management* provides a framework to support the Cybersecurity Challenge with consultants and periodic updates.
	Project Management supports the Cybersecurity Challenge project from a business administration point of view.

Table 2. Sequencing of Courses in the Masters of Cybersecurity and Leadership Program

Didactic Processes: Innovations in the MCL Classes

Several innovations in how these courses are taught represent the fifth internal element in the KBP Pedagogical Model. Specifically, these pedagogical innovations create a rich and meaningful experience for students that help veterans transition. Below we summarize the major activities and the kinds of experiences that help veterans learn about cybersecurity and about the business world outside of the military.

Industry Professionals. Throughout the program, faculty members invite guest speakers that are experts in their field, in particular leaders in business with the responsibility of protecting an organization's information security assets, such as Chief Information Security Officers (CISOs) from major corporations. The incorporation of industry professionals helps ensure that students both see the big picture, develop an appreciation for the type of careers available, and have an opportunity to ask these leading experts relevant questions related to cybersecurity and management. Students are encouraged to add these industry experts to their growing network of professional contacts. This is particularly important for veterans who may not have many contacts in the civilian world. In the cybersecurity domain, individuals work most effectively through collaboration and partnerships - not isolation. Thus, the inclusion of guest speakers that are experts in their field and offer varying viewpoints is of paramount importance to a career that demands an interdisciplinary and holistic approach to security (Endicott-Popovsky & Popovsky, 2014). Having students add these experts to their own professional network helps ensure this is carried forward from the classroom to their eventual careers in cybersecurity management.

Real-World Information Assurance Strategies. A major theme of the program is the development of student expertise in the area of information security and risk management. Students examine real world cases studies in information assurance and this provides the background for students to become future managers. These future mangers will be charged with responsibility for making decisions about the security of information systems. Since there is no 100% secure system and since there are not unlimited budgets to spend on securing systems, choices must be made about how, where, and when to invest in security. Students practice methods and techniques for applying industry methodology to problems in information assurance. Mastering this material will make the information assurance professional a better executive. Students develop an understanding of information assurance applied research, executive presentation of topics, and financial drivers for budgets and decision making. Students also practice developing and maintaining risk assessments, risk management plans, auditing, and enforcing policies and procedures. Parts of the program are based on the education and training standards of the Committee on National Security Systems certifications CNSS 4012, Senior System Manager (National Security Agency 2013).

Hands' on Experiences through Virtual Labs. Proprietary virtual lab environments have been developed by program faculty, which give students hands-on experience. One set of labs used in the network and internet security class helps students learn security policy design, incident response, and techniques to defend against, react to, and recover from a cyber-attack. Students conduct comprehensive laboratory exercises on internet protocols, reconnaissance, scanning, vulnerability assessment, and system hardening in a virtual network. These labs are designed with natural relationships among common phases of the attacks and defense technologies, providing students the opportunity to design and implement their own systems that meet a given security policy. Virtual Box is used to emulate the hardware of a computer and

different operating systems (e.g., Windows XP and Windows 7 virtual
machines). These virtual labs enrich students' experiences in operating and
managing various network systems and applications with minimal operating
and maintenance costs.

Engagement with the Non-Technical Business World. In addition to a
curriculum that links students' coursework to problems in the business world
and pays explicit attention to exposing students to the language and concepts
involved in business and management, the students benefit from the affiliation
with the Milgard School of Business in a variety of other ways. In particular,
they are able to engage in activities and events that connect them to Milgard
Master in Business Administration students and to local private sector
employers. For example, students in the MCL program are invited to the
annual Milgard Professional Networking Event where they learn useful tips on
how to build their professional network and engage in several rounds of speed
networking. They also are invited to the quarterly Executive Speaker Series
where they can benefit from hearing regional business leaders talk about their
organizations and experiences. These experiences help to forge informal
relationships between students in both programs as well as with private sector
employers.

Engagement in the Technical Business World. Students in the MCL
program attend the annual South Sound Technology Conference (SST),
which is hosted annually by the Institute of Technology at UWT. The SST is
a technology showcase for the South Puget Sound (Cooper 2013), and since
2000 it has brought together leaders from industry, education, and government
from around the state to discuss and demonstrate technological innovations
and their ongoing applications. Panel and keynote presentations – including
networking opportunities – provide a venue to discuss, explore, understand,
and deploy technology as a solution, an opportunity, and as an advantage.
Sessions planned for the South Sound Technology Conference have included
discussions on mobile application development, energy and sustainability,
information technology, and cybersecurity. Throughout the conference,
graduate and undergraduate students from the Institute of Technology
showcase their work through poster sessions and demonstrations in the gallery

area. Students get to interact with members of industry and industry participants can observe potential employees in a relaxed atmosphere.

Cybersecurity Capstone Challenge. A capstone course is a culminating experience for students in the program which gives them an opportunity to apply what they have learned in the classroom and gain valuable experience. Regional business leaders collaborate with program faculty to pose a relevant and interesting problem for a team of graduate students to solve in a three-month period. Past cybersecurity challenges are presented in Table 3. The benefits of the Cybersecurity Capstone Challenge include: 1) giving students the opportunity to apply their cybersecurity studies to real world issues and to receive valuable experience; 2) giving companies a motivated team at no cost; 3) enabling both students and company employees to expand their professional networks, thus increasing the opportunities to future employment, and 4) increasing the companies' engagement with UWT and the broader security community.

1) Communications Company wants their Unified Communications environment tested against a National Vulnerability Database.

2) An Internet security company desires a team to do a controlled assessment inside their Threat Intelligence Lab and link the results to the network defense team.

3) A software company wants to create an approach to embed security in applications development. A second project requests the student team create industry security guidance by assisting a team of developers in writing a protocol for emerging technologies.

4) A local county IT department wants a Critical Security Control Audit to evaluate how the county is adhering to Critical Security Controls. The student team will be working with the full-time county team.

5) A local port wants to harden its cybersecurity position based on the NIST Framework. The student team will work in tandem with the port IT staff and other stakeholders.

6) A local utility company desires the establishment of a policy to support the Cybersecurity Framework for Critical Infrastructure.

7) cybersecurity consulting firm will have a student team work alongside seasoned professionals and be guided in the use of assessment tools, risk analysis, and multiple commercial technologies used with cybersecurity consulting sessions.

Table 3. Cybersecurity Challenges

EXTENDING THE KBP MODEL TO INCORPORATE ORGANIZATIONAL DESIGN

Above, we have used the KBP model to describe three external contextual elements (new students, job market, and trends) that together shape the five internal elements of the MCL program (students, teachers, content, goals, and didactic processes) and have explained how this pedagogical system helps the veteran transition to the civilian workplace. Classes are taught at night on a full-time basis so the transitioning veteran can use their educational benefits to attend and can still work full time if need be. The cohort structure of the program design helps to develop a supportive learning community, one in which veterans are directly interacting and learning from their fellow students, many of whom come from business organizations outside the military. Class content is designed in a way to expose veterans to the cultures and practices of the business world and to connect their leadership and managerial experience to this business world. Innovations in course design enable the veteran to learn about careers in cybersecurity and to network with cybersecurity professionals.

Using the KBP Model has allowed us to identify broad environmental contextual elements as well as very specific curricular elements that shape pedagogical design of a program that uniquely serves the transitioning veteran. However, our experience with the MCL reveals three additional considerations relating the organizational and administrative context that are important to the program's ongoing ability to effectively integrate broad environmental inputs to the curriculum and pedagogy. We have identified three examples of organizational design elements: 1) the need for formal structural linkages that institutionalize the ongoing engagement and involvement between two separate campus units; 2) the creation of control processes that include the monitoring and collection of data on students and their learning outcomes over time, and 3) the integration of a recruiter and advisor with military expertise. This third organizational design element is particularly critical in terms of recruiting the right kind of veteran student, helping that student to adjust and connect to other services on campus that might benefit them, and providing real-time information to faculty who are responsible for the content of the curriculum.

Institutionalizing Linkages between Programs. Because this is a joint program between two different departments of a university, ongoing administration and governance processes had to be established that support and maintain the interdisciplinary content of the curriculum. A joint venture between two programs on a campus requires faculty and administration to move beyond their own siloed perspectives and to discover shared areas of interest. A key element for success is the establishment of forums for regular dialogue between faculty from the Institute of Technology and the Milgard School of Business. Quarterly program meetings were established to coordinate and improve the linkages between courses and to discuss students' progress towards program learning outcomes. New governance vehicles and procedures for managing the curriculum were also established. A committee comprised of faculty teaching in the MCL program from both schools is charged with overseeing admissions and developing the curriculum; however, votes among each respective faculty are still taken when required by faculty code.

Creation of Control Systems for Continuous Improvement. Assessment and monitoring of the program and the students' experience enables faculty to be responsive to student needs, especially in the early days. Formally, students are given a survey at the end of every course to assess how to improve each course. Informally, periodic discussion groups are used to gauge student morale and to assess what they are getting out of the classes. Such data collected in the first year revealed a serious deficiency in students' incoming knowledge of basic business concepts, and resulted in the alteration of one of the first classes into what is now the Business Essentials class, a survey oriented class to acclimate students to the world of business. As the program matures and prompted in part by accreditation requirements for the Milgard School of Business, the MCL faculty committee is developing an outcomes assessment process that identifies instruments and measures to assess student learning (the program learning goals and objectives); collects, analyzes, and disseminates the assessment information, and uses that information for continuous improvement of the program (c.f., AACSB Assurance of Learning Standards: An Interpretation, 2013).

Integrating Recruiting and Advising Functions. An additional program level organizational consideration relates to the structure of administering the program and how those administrative roles are integrated with ongoing curricular design and modification. The MCL program employs a full-time recruiter and advisor who markets the program and serves the local pool of potential students coming from a military background. While there are active duty officers and senior enlisted seeking a master's degree for promotional purposes, many service members are preparing for retirement or forced transition to civilian careers as a result of the drawdown cycle. Thus, the presence of a dedicated recruiter and advisor who understands these dynamics is critical to the program's success. Encouraging these mid-career professionals through the application process, guiding them through the Graduate Record Exam (GRE), and supporting them as they face a transition from military to academic culture builds rapport, trust, and goodwill in the community. During the application process, the advisor identifies immediate and long-term career goals. While they are in the program, students receive individualized coaching sessions and workshops enabling them to achieve their goals. Such individual attention increases enrollment as well as retention, two key factors in determining the success of a program. In addition, through relationships with the existing students, the recruiter also provides important feedback to faculty on how the program is serving veterans that feed forward into additional adjustments to the curriculum and to individual faculty's pedagogical practices.

Curriculum design does not occur independent of the organizational structures in which it operates, and these three elements have a direct bearing on the degree to which the pedagogical system can take new veteran students and process them into cybersecurity leaders over time. This level of elements influencing pedagogical design connects the broad environment to the students, faculty, curriculum, and the organization, leading us to suggest revisions to the KBP Model. Our experience at UWT provides three concrete examples of organizational design considerations that link the broad environmental inputs to the specific internal components of the pedagogical system. However, depending on the program and university, other structural organizational design elements might exist that similarly shape and provide feedback to the pedagogical system, including student mental health centers, learning centers, and other centralized student services that exist on a university campus. Figure 2 incorporates the concept of organizational level design elements in the existing KBP Model and shows how this level feeds into and receives feedback from the central internal elements of pedagogical design.

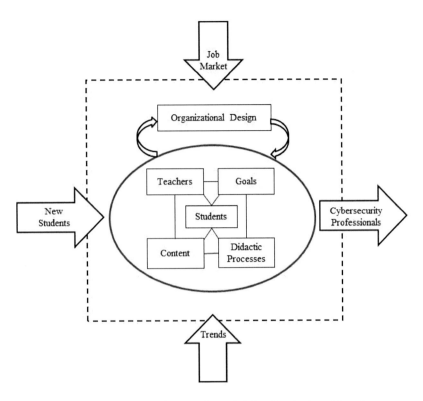

Figure 2. Revised KBP Pedagogical Model for Curriculum Development

In summary, the MCL is a dynamic and vibrant graduate degree program that serves a local and regional community by bringing together academia, community leaders, military, and public and private organizations. The KBP Model is a useful tool for integrating both external contextual considerations relating to inputs of such a program as well as the internal factors that directly relate to the pedagogy and curriculum of a program. For transitioning military personnel in particular, the design of this program enables transitioning veterans to combine the knowledge, skills, and abilities from their military careers with the business and technical acumen so that they may successfully transition into civilian careers that are in high demand. Our test case reveals the importance of including explicit reference to organizational design considerations that further shape the pedagogical system. Institutionalizing the relationships between two separate academic units on campus, creating formal control systems that regularly assess and provide feedback on learning outcomes, and integrating dedicated in-house advisors with military expertise to inform faculty on issues related to this population ensures that the pedagogical system functions effectively over time and is responsive to the needs of the cybersecurity field and to our veteran students.

REFERENCES

[1] AACSB Assurance of Learning Standards: An Interpretation. (2013.) Retrieved from http://www.aacsb.edu/~/media/AACSB/Publications/white-papers/wp-assurance-of-learning-standards.ashx.

[2] Ashton, A. (2015). JBLM Airmen Share Memories as They Prep for Squadron's Shutdown, The Olympian, Jan 12. Retrieved from http://www.theolympian.com/2015/01/12/3522436/this-is-what-the-drawdown-looks.html

[3] Ashton, A. (2014). Community Leaders Rally to Protect JBLM Workforce. The News Tribune, Dec. 29. Retrieved from http://www.military.com/daily-news/2014/12/29/community-leaders-rally-to-protect-jblm-workforce.html

[4] Clemens, E. V., & Milsom, A. S. (2008). Enlisted Service Members' Transition Into the Civilian World of Work: A Cognitive Information Processing Approach. Career Development Quarterly, 56(3), 246-256.

[5] Cooper K. (2013). Hundreds Discuss Mobile Web, Data Security at University of Washington Tacoma's South Sound Technology Conference (2013). Retrieved from http://www.tacoma.uw.edu/events/south-sound-technology-conference

[6] Cybersecurity Forum Initiative - CSFI (2014). Senior Cyber Leadership – Why a Technically Competent Cyber Workforce is Not Enough. Retrieved from http://www.csfi.us/?page=reports

[7] Endicott-Popovsky, B., Popovsky, V. (2014). Application of Pedagogical Fundamentals for the Holistic Development of Cybersecurity Professionals. ACM Inroads. Vol. 5, No. 1.

[8] George Washington University (2013). Program Requirements of the Master of Cybersecurity in Computer Science. Retrieved from http://www.cs.gwu.edu/academics/graduate_programs/master/cybersecurity/program-requirements

[9] Goda, B., Friedman R. (2012). Designing a Masters Program in Cybersecurity and Leadership.

[10] Retrieved from http://sigite2012.sigite.org/wp-content/uploads/2012/08/session01-paper02.pdf

[11] Gjelten, T. (2013). Cyber Warrior Shortage Threatens U.S. Security. Retrieved from National Public Radio http://www.npr.org/templates/story/story.php?storyId=128574055s

[12] Harris, S. (2012) *Certified Information Systems Security Professional Exam Guide, 6th Edition.* New York. McGraw Hill Professional.

[13] International Information Systems Security Certification Consortium (2014). Certified Information Systems Security Professional. Retrieved from https://www.isc2.org/CISSP/Default.aspx

[14] Ma, M. (2015). Mark Pagano Selected as Chancellor of UW Tacoma. UW Today, Jan 6. http://www.washington.edu/news/2015/01/06/mark-pagano-selected-as-chancellor-of-uw-tacoma/

[15] Obama, B. (2009).Obama at the Academy IV: Speech Text. Retrieved from http://news.sciencemag.org/2009/04/obama-academy-iv-speech-text.

[16] Roman, J. (2012). The New IT Security Skills Set. Retrieved from http://www.bankinfosecurity.com/new-security-skills-set-a-5022/op-1

[17] Simpson, A. s., & Armstrong, S. s. (2009). From the Military to the Civilian Work Force: Addressing Veteran Career Development Concerns. Career Planning & Adult Development Journal, 25(1), 177-187.

[18] Stone, C. and Stone, D. (2014). Factors affecting hiring decisions about veterans, Human Resource Management Review, Volume 25, Issue 1, March 2015, Pages 68-79, ISSN 1053-4822, http://dx.doi.org/10.1016/j.hrmr.2014.06.003.

VetsEngr: Easing Student Veterans' Transition to Cybersecurity Careers

Elizabeth J. Moore, Ph.D.
Applied Inference
Seattle Washington

Viatcheslav M. Popovsky, Ph.D.
HERD Department
University of Idaho

Barbara Endicott-Popovsky, Ph.D.
Institute of Technology
University of Washington Tacoma

In 2010 and 2011 The VetsEngr Project, a pilot program funded by the National Science Foundation [1] , studied Washington National Guard enrollment in the Information Security and Risk Management (ISRM) certificate offered at the University of Washington through continuing education. Inspired by the 2009 NSF report, *Veteran's Education for Engineering and Science*[2], and motivated by a STEM planning grant[3], VetsEngr sought to identify barriers service members face in transitioning to academia in pursuit of careers in cybersecurity.

VetsEngr was the basis for developing an assessment tool for identifying those individuals most likely to succeed in a cybersecurity education program and, ultimately, a career. With the U.S. facing a serious shortage of

---

[1] National Science Foundation. (2010-2012). [EEC 1037814] VetsEngr Project, PI Barbara Endicott-Popovsky, Co-PI Amelia Phillips Highline Community College.
[2] National Science Foundation. (2009). "Veterans' Education for Engineering and Science." This study identified the opportunity to leverage technical military training and aptitudes to support service members' transition to civilian careers via postsecondary education.
[3] Rajala, S. (2009). NSF #0951441: "A Planning Grant Proposal for Transitioning America's Veterans to Science, Technology, Engineering and Mathematics Academic Programs," Mississippi State University.

cybersecurity professionals, many military personnel, eligible for generous educational benefits, have already received military training and experience that could be transferred to cybersecurity careers as civilians. This is especially true in the Pacific Northwest where the Guard draws from local technology companies such as Amazon, Boeing, Microsoft and T-Mobile.

Interested service members were invited to participate in the Risk Management and Information Assurance certificate program. The program had both an in class and an online component.

METHOD

Five service members participated in a focus group in Lakewood, WA on March 29, 2011 to share their experiences in attempting to use their educational benefits, and suggestions for overcoming any barriers identified. The Nominal Group Technique (NGT) was used. The two probe questions asked were:

1) What are all the barriers, internal and external, that prevent military personnel from using their education benefits (to prepare for STEM careers)?

2) What are all the ideas you can think of that would help overcome those barriers?

When using the NGT, individuals are given about five minutes to record all the answers they can. Then one-by-one, participants are asked to read one of their responses. This continues until the last participant has exhausted his/her list. "Hitchhiking" is encourage, meaning that if new ideas occur to the participants as they hear responses from their peers, they are encouraged to add them to their list. The benefit of this approach is that the period of individual responding, followed by "hitchhiking" tends to result in a broader array of responses than a traditional focus group approach.

One of the ideas mentioned during this process was the creation of a campus "Honor House," modeled after Canadian programs that were developed to support their veterans. A third phase of the focus group entailed an "Idea-writing" exercise responding to the instruction: Design Your Ideal and Sustainable Honor House. Each participant responded to this instruction with his or her preliminary design in about 5 minutes. When completed, the participants traded with one another, read the other person's design and modified it to incorporate their concepts. This process continued until each participant had the opportunity to respond to each design.

FINDINGS

Nominal Group Technique question 1:

What are all the barriers, internal and external, that prevent military personnel from using their education benefits (to prepare for STEM careers)?

The challenges identified by this group focused on a lack of awareness related to how to work with the educational benefits, including a lack of familiarity and a bureaucratic inflexibility on the part of the institutions, and a lack of awareness on the part of the service member about the different programs, opportunities, and requirements.

The three top barriers identified by this group are:

- the ongoing struggle inherent in working with two complex bureaucracies (the UW and the military) that are not well integrated

- the lack of awareness on the part of the service members as to educational opportunities and the benefits for which they are eligible

- the service member's need to work because of the costs that are not covered by the GI bill. This barrier, combined with the understanding that some benefits are available only for full time students, means that service members who do not have other support may not be eligible for some of the GI bill's benefits.

In addition to these top three barriers, participants identified other categories of barriers, including:

- **Personal barriers** that might interfere with a service member's use of educational benefits, including inadequate educational preparation (or fear of this), family responsibilities, disabilities (including PTSD which might interfere with learning), or lack of geographic access;

- **Lack of career planning** including not knowing how to translate a military skill into a civilian job, a lack of long-term career planning, and no clear understanding of career pathways and the education or training required to travel those pathways.

- **Cultural differences** between the military and the postsecondary setting, including differences in values, the chaos that can be found in a university setting relative to a more orderly military setting, and no place for service members to assemble on campus to create a community.

Nominal Group Technique Question 2:

What are all the ideas you can think of that would help overcome those barriers?

The suggestions proposed by the participants focused on 1) simplifying and otherwise increasing the accessibility of the benefits system; 2) changes to the system to increase articulation between military training and postsecondary credits, and to improve the payment process; 3) creating support procedures within the military so that career planning and use of educational benefits becomes an obligation of the military rather than just an option for the service member, and within the academic institution.

Simplified, accessible system: One individual suggested a system that would enable him to enter his social security number and receive a report about his education benefits. He noted that retirement benefits are reported using such a system. Another suggested an electronic checklist (with contact information for each step) that constitutes a step-by-step process for navigating the pathway from the military, through the academic institution, into a civilian career.

System integration: Participants suggested establishing identified articulated pathways so that service members with certain training can apply for academic credit based on that training. For some, this would mean shortening the academic program and for others, it would help the service member know how they might transition their skills from the military to civilian life. Participants suggested workshops where academic staff and military education personnel "get on the same page" and get to know each other. They also suggested improvements in the payment process, both linking what the military will pay with what the academic institution will charge, and meeting the institution's payment schedule.

Support: Participants suggested a shift in the commitment of the military to the future careers of their service members. They suggested making it an obligation of the military to counsel and support service members in this way from their first day and increasingly through the discharge process. One specifically requested that a counselor be available to take a call when the veteran begins to encounter roadblocks in the process of accessing the educational benefits. In addition to enhanced support on the military side, participants suggested enhanced support on the academic side as well. Suggestions included bringing classes to the post, creating a mentorship system with service members or veterans who have already made it through, making the campus veterans' centers more helpful, and creating a place where service members can form a community and support one another.

Appendix I contains flip chart notes organized into response categories for both NGT questions.

Idea writing: Design your ideal and sustainable Honor House.

Participants agreed that the Honor House should be located on or near campus and feel warm, comfortable, welcoming, and accepting, and visually reminiscent of the military ("with an educational twist"). Their design would include:

- a kitchen and dining area
- common areas for gathering together and hosting guest speakers, workshops and celebrations
- places for small groups to meet and study together
- independent study facilities

- access to the library, computers, and the Internet, as well as a textbook exchange.

Participants recommended offering basic services through a combination of paid staff and volunteers, preferably veterans themselves. Staff should provide psychological services; expert advice on paperwork for military students in general, and financial aid in particular; career counseling and navigation: and academic support and tutoring. Staff should be able to respond to service-specific issues, and be prepared to address the needs of veterans with disabilities. Volunteers and alumni would be invited to serve as mentors, tutors, or in other support roles.

RECOMMENDATIONS

- Prioritize career planning and education for service members: Make career thinking, counseling, and planning part of the service's ongoing message to service members from basic training to discharge. Track educational attainment by service members at the unit level as an outcome so that more attainment is rewarded.

- Make educational benefits more accessible: until a system similar to that used for retirement benefits is available, service members will need to rely on experts within the military or within academia to help them navigate the complex benefits, complex educational systems, and transfer of credits from military training to civilian training to convert their career planning to actual education. This may require an educational "navigator" housed on base or at the educational institution or elsewhere.

- Identify several likely military-to-civilian career transitions and work toward establishing pathways to those civilian careers with specific institutions. This would include an identified course of study, and articulation agreements spelling out how credits will transfer from the military to the academic setting.

- Establish a structure for service members and veterans to meet, study together, and support one another through their education and into their career. This community should be welcoming and accessible for all service members, at any stage in their career path.

- Encourage communication and collaboration between the military education center staff and academic staff.

CONCLUSIONS

Findings from this pilot confirm the major findings from the 2009 NSF study, Veterans' Education for Engineering and Science which suggests that special programs need to be established to assist veterans transitioning to academic programs – particularly those in STEM fields of study. While we know that many military occupations fall into the science and technology areas, this does not always translate into pursuit of STEM fields of study. For example, in 2009, less than one percent of young veterans work in the information and communication industry 24 months after they exit the military; however, approximately thirty-five percent of enlisted members serve in electronics, communications, or other technical fields.[4] This would suggest that some facilitation within the academic environment is necessary to assist these veterans in being successful in technical fields of study. This facilitation should also include finding ways to fully support the veterans and their families during summers between academic years. The GI Bill offers 36 months of academic support – which translates to four years of nine-month support. Veterans need a more comprehensive support program that will provide four years of twelve-month support.

The findings from this study have become the basis for a transition support program at the University of Washington Tacoma that includes not only academic programs in cybersecurity oriented toward veterans, but also the support systems necessary to ensure successful completion and re-entry into the work place.

The insights from this study have led to the creation of CREATES, the Cybersecurity Rapid Education and Transition to Employment System, that integrates many of the ideas that emerged from the pilot. This program is currently being implemented at the university and resources from the community organized to feed the system. See figure 1.

---

[4] Ibid. Rajala, S. (2009).

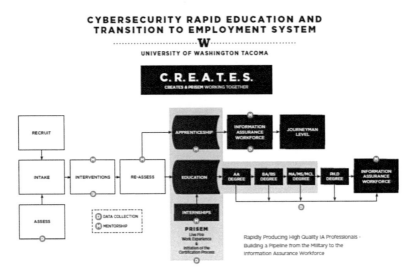

Figure 1. CREATES Pipeline (Source: Morgan Zantua, MS)

The system begins with intake that includes a recruiting and assessment process. Interventions are identified and the transitioning student's readiness is re-assessed. Education is complemented by both apprenticeships and internships that complement and amplify student learning in preparation for careers following graduation. Students are able to select a path from 2-yr programs through graduate degrees prior to emerging in the workforce. Choice of a path is aided by a database, under development, of degree offerings through NSA/DHS Centers of Academic Excellence across the country, knowing that only 40% of the 8,000 per year of veterans transitioning through the Pacific Northwest will settle here.

Initial NSF funding resulting from the 2009 study of transitioning veterans into STEM disciplines launched this effort that is now addressing the needs of veterans returning through Joint Base Lewis McChord and Camp Murray. Agreements are being executed with military branches to assist with their transition efforts and to assure that returning military have opportunities to pursue careers in cybersecurity that are in demand.[5]

APPENDIX I

DETAILED FOCUS GROUP FINDINGS

NGT 1: What are all the barriers, internal and external, that prevent military personnel from using their education benefits (to prepare for STEM careers)?

Top three barriers

1) **★★Lack of awareness** about education system opportunities and benefits of GI bill

   a. Lots of different programs with different requirements – it's confusing

   b. "Convergence is happening with the programs"

   c. Complex benefit structure; mixed benefit sources

2) **★★Two difficult bureaucracies** that don't speak to each other (University and Military). It's labor intensive just to get through both systems. This is an ongoing struggle.

   a. Knowledge – paperwork – the process

   b. "Getting grades to the education department; doing the paperwork"

   c. Motivation energy to get through systems – it's exhausting

   d. Universities are not adapted to veterans

---

[5] Army Reserve Launches Partnership to Create Pathway for Cyber Warriors," U.S. Army Reserve web site, Feb. 12, 2015, http://www.usar.army.mil/resources/Pages/Army-Reserve-launches-partnership-to-create-pathway-for-cyber-warriors.aspx

e. Articulation for life experiences – postsecondary institutions can't translate experience from military to college credit. (Some know how; some don't.)

3) **Conflict with job** – need to work because costs aren't covered. But some benefits are available only for fulltime students.

    a. Out of pocket cost – FTA doesn't cover 100%

    b. Have to pay for books

Personal, internal barriers

    a. Educational preparation (maybe just a GED)
    b. Fear, intimidation, self-doubt about academic performance in the past.
    c. Family responsibilities
    d. Physical and mental barriers – PTSD might block a soldier's wanting to enter life or might be a roadblock to learning
    e. Maturity and persistence of military personnel
    f. Geographic access, transportation barriers
    g. College isn't their goal

Lack of Career planning

    a. Lack of a sense of long term career planning – emergency mentality

    b. Unawareness of civilian job context – how to translate my skill into a civilian job

    c. Lack of clear career pathway through education

Cultural differences

    a. Cultural difference between military environment and values/ and college environment and values – liberal vs. conservative

    b. Chaotic university setting

    c. Unknown university setting

    d. No place to assemble on campus

NGT 2: What are all the ideas you can think of that would help overcome those barriers?

Simplified, accessible system

a. Want a program that takes my SSN and knows my education benefits (like retirement benefits)

b. And send that info to educational institution

c. Simplification. Electronic checklist – benefits and a step by step process that takes you through the process. A roadmap. Who you call. Step 1, step 2, step 3.

System integration

a. Identified pathways aligned with what military people do and have already earned credits toward (part of orientation system).

b. Establish articulation process

c. Workshops with military educational personnel and academic personnel – get on same page, have same standards – and get to know each other – create better partnerships

d. VA office on campus has to be prepared – they must be more aggressive for the soldiers

e. Jump start funding (don't have to wait for funding)

f. Figure out what military will pay and institution will charge that. Cater to the military

Support

a. Change the system so that it is an obligation of the military, not just an option for the service member. Orientation process while in the military – get the service members thinking about possibilities for their future, their career, and their education. Measure it by outcome, not output. Individualized career planning.

b. Informed employment counselors (embed education opportunities into soldier on exit – a beefed up ACAP)/ informed deployment personnel.

        i.   Counselor must personally offer assistance (call me if you need help)

c. Authorize more benefits for full time students

d. Place/Community

        i.   Move classrooms to the army post

       ii.   Web Ex classes

     iii.   Place to assemble, like a fraternity house

     iv.   Have all this at veteran's center on campus/ focal points of information

      v.   Mentorship for service members (military who are ahead or academic people)

21465302R00113

Made in the USA
Middletown, DE
30 June 2015